William J. Walsh

Bimetallism and Monometallism

What they are and how they bear upon the Irish land question

William J. Walsh

Bimetallism and Monometallism
What they are and how they bear upon the Irish land question

ISBN/EAN: 9783744735223

Printed in Europe, USA, Canada, Australia, Japan

Cover: Foto ©Thomas Meinert / pixelio.de

More available books at **www.hansebooks.com**

'lism and Monometal'

BIMETALLISM

AND

MONOMETALLISM:

WHAT THEY ARE, AND HOW THEY BEAR UPON

THE IRISH LAND QUESTION.

BY

THE MOST REV. DR. WALSH,

Archbishop of Dublin.

BROWNE & NOLAN,

NASSAU-STREET, DUBLIN,

Printers and Publishers.

1893.

CONTENTS.

INTRODUCTION.

IN this pamphlet is reproduced, in a considerably expanded form, an Interview recently published in a Dublin newspaper.[1]

I endeavoured in that Interview to direct attention to the disastrous effects of our present monetary system upon the farmers of Ireland. I had in view, especially, those whose rents have been judicially fixed for 15 years under the provisions of the Land Act of 1881, and —in a still higher degree—those who are under the obligation of making fixed annual payments to the State for a term of 49 years, from having purchased their farms under one or other of the Land Purchase Acts of recent years.

Throughout I have borne in mind the words of Mr. Ottomar Haupt, who, a few years ago, in his work on " Bimetallic England," wrote as follows :—

" The actual working of Bimetallism . . . in our days has never been touched upon in a tangible way.

" What we possess is a mass of literature of an abstract kind, in which the discussions on Money, on Standard, on Currency, on Value, and so on, play the main part, and are treated in so complicated a way that the reader loses himself in the niceties of Political Economy."[2]

Those words, indeed, are no longer applicable in their

---

[1] See the *Freeman's Journal and National Press* (Dublin), 28th Nov. 1892.
[2] *Bimetallic England*, by Ottomar Haupt (quoted by Sir Guilford L. Molesworth, in his Prize Essay, *Silver and Gold : the Money of the World* : Effingham Wilson, London, 1891, page 79.)

fulness to the existing literature of the currency question. But, even yet, I venture to say, they are applicable to it in some degree. Many publications, indeed, both large and small, have of late years issued from the press, in explanation of the general bearings of the controversy between Monometallists and Bimetallists, or in advocacy of either of their conflicting views. In this way, much has been done to clear away the haze of obscurity and confusion in which the controversy was involved. Yet I feel justified in thinking that there still is room for an attempt, such as I have thought of making, to bring the subject before the public in a form in which it may without difficulty be understood by every intelligent reader.

To anyone who has read my Interview as published in newspaper form, it would be superfluous to point out what was the chief aim and drift of all that I said in it.

But here, by way of introduction, I may remark that, first and before all else, I directed attention to the increasing hardship of the position in which—as the result of the existing monetary arrangements of England and of a large portion of the commercial world—the farmers of Ireland are placed by certain incidents of the remedial land legislation of the last twelve or thirteen years.

Furthermore, I directed attention to the fact that it is the State, and the State alone, that must bear the full weight of responsibility for the maintenance of those monetary arrangements, under which even that eminently beneficent legislation, instead of being a source of permanent good, has become a source of grave anxiety, and possibly of disaster, to those in whose behalf it was introduced.

It is not, I think, out of place for me to state that, in view of the fact that I said all this very plainly, I have read not without surprise some words of striking eulogy in which, on a recent public occasion, my treatment of the subject was spoken of by a prominent English politician who has not hitherto been regarded as a sympathiser with the tenant-farmers of Ireland either in their past or in their present struggles with the severe and ever-increasing difficulties of their position.

I refer, of course, to the speech delivered at the opening of the recent National Agricultural Conference in London, by the Right Hon. H. Chaplin, Minister for Agriculture in the late Conservative Ministry. In that speech Mr. Chaplin expressed a hope that my views, expressed in the newspaper report of my Interview, might be "embodied in a pamphlet, and distributed broadcast among the agriculturalists of England."[1]

Partly in view of the wish thus expressed, but mainly in compliance with a joint request which came to me from a number of the delegates recently assembled at the International Monetary Congress at Brussels, I have prepared the Interview for republication in pamphlet form.

In all the criticisms that I have met with upon my Interview—sympathetic or unsympathetic as they may have been—I find that there is one point as to which no exception has been taken. No one has said that I have not made my meaning plain.

[1] Speech at the National Agricultural Conference in St. James's Hall, London, Dec. 7th, 1892 (*Daily News* report).

For this favourable judgment I have to thank the leniency of my critics. I must, however, add that if they are satisfied upon this point, I am not. On a careful revision of my Interview, I have found in it some things that are not put at all so plainly as they might have been. In now republishing it, I have done my best to clear it of this drawback.

I have also inserted some observations on several points of importance not originally touched upon. And I have added—for the most part in their own words—some statements of the views of those who have written upon various aspects of the subject in hand. I have done this in most cases in which I have been able to find in the works of those writers a passage sufficiently free from technicalities to be suitable for insertion in a statement such as this. For I have always had to bear in mind that I am writing mainly for those who may wish to know something of the merits of the Bimetallist controversy, but who have to approach the subject without being in any way acquainted with the principles, or even with the phraseology, of the science of Political Economy.

Some newspaper correspondence, and other discussions to which the publication of my Interview has given rise, suggest to me the advisability of here making a few further remarks upon the subject of Bimetallism in its general bearings.

I. It has been assumed by some impulsive critics that Bimetallism is put forward by its advocates as an absolute panacea for all the evils of our present social state.

Criticism based upon so mistaken a view is, of

course, altogether wide of the mark. As Mr. Knox, M.P. recently wrote :—

" I notice that [a correspondent] wishes to know how Bimetallism would cure all the evils of depression. It won't. No single thing will. Anybody who says one single reform will cure all our trouble is to be distrusted . . .

" Whether rents are reduced or not, whether Home Rule is passed or not, we shall have to face the currency difficulty. But, on the other hand, if we adopted Bimetallism, not merely would the need for Home Rule remain unaffected, but many aspects of the agricultural depression might remain uncured.

" Bimetallism is one of the things necessary to set us on our legs again, but only one of them." [1]

II. It has also been assumed that Bimetallism is something new, a mere craze of some eccentric theorists of the latter half of this nineteenth century.

One or two critics have taken this strangely erroneous assumption as their starting-point.

Their mistake, as they ought to have been able to see for themselves, was provided against beforehand in the Interview itself.

It was stated there, in the plainest possible words, that, so far from Bimetallism being a novelty, the very contrary is the case.[2] It is not Bimetallism, but Monometallism, that is the novelty. Even in England, Monometallism is of modern introduction. England, of old, was a Bimetallist country, and did not abandon Bimetallism until 1816. In France, in Italy, in Belgium, in Switzerland, and in other countries of Europe,

---

[1] Letter in the *Freeman's Journal and National Press* (Dublin), Dec. 3rd, 1892.
[2] See page 27.

Bimetallism was in full operation until 1873. It was the maintenance of Bimetallism in so many European countries during the years from 1816 to 1873, that practically secured for England and for the rest of the commercial world, throughout those years, all the main advantages of the Bimetallic system.[1]

Bimetallism, then, is in no sense novel. On the contrary, it is the abandonment of the Bimetallic system, as that system was worked in France and elsewhere[2] until 1873, that has to be looked upon as a venturesome experiment. That experiment has been made, and, as has now become evident, the result has been anything but a success.

III. I next come to a more serious error.

It has been assumed that the existence or non-existence of the gigantic and ever-growing burden, which, as I explained in my Interview,[3] now presses so heavily upon the farmers of Ireland, is a matter merely of argument—a thing to be affirmed if we adopt the Bimetallist view of the currency question, and to be denied if we adopt the view of the Monometallists.

This is a grievous mistake.

Whether (a) as to the existence of that burden, or (b) as to its oppressiveness, or (c) as to the fact that it is a burden which is ever growing heavier and heavier, there is no room for doubt, if there is evidence that, owing to the recent and present position of affairs in the commercial world, gold has risen, and is rising, and must continue to rise, in value.

The connection between these two sets of facts is indisputable, and it is universally recognised as indisputable. A rise in the value of gold means an addition

---

[1] See pages 31-33.   [2] See page 28.
[3] See pages 45, 46 ; 51-56.

to the burden that presses upon every farmer. A continuous rise in the value of gold means a constantly increasing addition to that burden.[1] These are propositions which cannot be denied or called in question by any one who knows the meaning of the words that he is using.

What question, then, can be supposed to remain open? Simply the question of fact, whether or not gold has risen, and is continuing to rise, in value. But neither is this any longer a really open question. That gold has risen, that it is rising, and that in all probability it must continue to rise in value, is now recognised no less distinctly by Monometallists[2] than it is by Bimetallists.

The only practical difference between Monometallists and Bimetallists as to this point is, that Bimetallists have a practical remedy to suggest—their suggestion being that certain currency arrangements which were abandoned in 1873 should now be revived[3]—whilst the Monometallists have no practical remedy to suggest, and, in effect, give up the whole case in despair.[4]

As for recognising that the evil exists, and that it is an evil of serious and even alarming gravity, there is no difference whatever between the two contending schools.

For a reason that will presently appear, it is of the utmost practical importance that this point should be kept distinctly in view.[5]

IV. It has furthermore been assumed by some commentators upon my Interview, that a belief in the possibility of establishing a fixed ratio of value between gold and silver is a sort of touchstone of Bimetallist orthodoxy.

[1] See page 45, 46.   [2] See pages 56-72.   [3] See page 28.
[4] See pages 92-96.   [5] See pages xi.–xiv.

I take the following as a specimen of the comments based upon that assumption :—

"The Monometallists reply that . . *you cannot fix the ratio between gold and silver*. . .

"His Grace the Archbishop of Dublin, it will be seen. is a *convinced Bimetallist. He thinks it is possible to fix a ratio* between the respective values of gold and silver."[1]

Now I may perhaps by some expressions in my Interview have made myself responsible for the error into which the writer of the passage I have just quoted was led. I have, therefore, in this Pamphlet taken special care to state,—not only clearly, but fully,—to what extent this point about the possibility of fixing a ratio between the value of silver and the value of gold comes into consideration as a matter in dispute.

Practically the point is not any longer in dispute at all.

There are, indeed, some few adherents of Monometallism, in an early but now rather antiquated form of that theory, who still maintain, as a fundamental article of the Monometallist creed, that it is not possible by any State regulation to keep the values of silver and gold at a fixed ratio.

That view of the case, however, has long since been abandoned by Monometallists as a school. It was not indeed possible for them, in the face of the indisputable facts of the case, to go on contending that the values of the two precious metals could not be kept at a fixed ratio.[2] Besides, on that point, the Report of the Gold and Silver Commission[3] of 1887 was fatally adverse to the old Monometallist view. Even the Monometallist members of that Commission did not venture to struggle against the

---

[1] *Freeman's Journal and National Press*, 28th November, 1892.
[2] See pages 60-62 ; 73-87.   [3] See page 38.

overwhelming force of the case that was made out by the facts in evidence before them. They withdrew, then, from the defence of the old high-and-dry position that it was impossible by State regulation to maintain a fixed ratio of value between gold and silver.[1] With their withdrawal from that position, the question of the possibility of maintaining such a ratio necessarily ceased to mark a dividing line between the Bimetallist and the Monometallist schools.

Some few Monometallists of the older type, such, for instance, as Mr. Giffen,[2] the official statistician of the Board of Trade, seem at times inclined still to hold by the Monometallist creed in its primitive form. From their point of view, indeed, they are not without reason for doing so. For they are sufficiently acute to see that in no other form is the theory of Monometallism really capable of being upheld even as a plausible topic of academic discussion.

But those adherents of Monometallism as it was understood in bygone days are no longer in the current of practical advocacy of the Monometallic cause. They have been left stranded by the receding tide. In disregard of all Mr. Giffen's clamorous protests,[3] Monometallists evidently have made up their minds no longer to burden themselves with the responsibility of defending ground which the investigations of the Gold and Silver Commission of 1887 have shown to be untenable.

V. This may be the most convenient place to call attention to an aspect of the case which seems, unaccountably, to have, as yet, attracted but little attention.

---

[1] See pages 78-83.   [2] See pages 84-86.   [3] Ibid.

If the Bimetallist view of the currency question is the true one, then these two things are clear beyond all possibility of question :—

1. The tenant-farmers of Ireland are at present placed in a position of grievous and increasing hardship ;[1] and,

2. The State, by its persistent maintenance of the present Monometallic system of currency—to say nothing of other grounds of responsibility—is directly responsible for the continuance of that hardship.

Many other interests—in England,[2] in India,[3] and elsewhere[4]—are oppressed by the maintenance of the present currency system. But in one respect the case of the Irish farmers stands almost alone.

In their case, the difficulty,—in so far as it is due to the working of Monometallism,—consists in this, that they are bound by a legal obligation to make certain fixed annual payments, the amounts of which are fixed by State authority, but which have now become notably more burdensome than they were when the State authority imposed them.[5]

Here, then, we have a two-fold responsibility fastened upon the State.

In the first place, the State is responsible for the maintenance of the currency system out of which the whole difficulty has grown.

In the second place, the State is responsible for the maintenance of the obligation,— imposed by its authority upon tenants and tenant-purchasers,—to make those fixed

---

[1] See pages 45-56. [2] See pages 33-37 ; 46-50
[3] See pages 37-42. [4] See pages 42, 43.
[5] See pages 45-56.

annual payments which, under the operation of the present currency system, have grown to be so oppressive.

The State, then, cannot free itself of its responsibilities towards Irish tenants and tenant-purchasers by a mere bald refusal to recognize Bimetallism as an effective means of remedying the existing grievance.

A thorough-going remedy, indeed, for that grievance seems possible only if the State will take courage to set to work upon the one logical basis of action—the replacing of its currency system upon Bimetallist lines.

But, it is said, the influence of the capitalists of the world is sufficiently potent to keep the way blocked against any such measure of reform.[1] If this be so,—as, unfortunately, it may be,—then, so far as Ireland is concerned, the duty of the Government of the country plainly lies in another direction.

What that direction is, there can be no difficulty in discovering. From all that has been said it clearly follows that, in view of the altered circumstances of the time, there is an urgent need for an equitable revision of the terms of all those annual payments, the terms of which have been fixed by State authority.

The obligation of making those annual payments *has its root exclusively in acts of the authority of the State.* In each individual case, the precise amount to be paid has been *fixed, or sanctioned, by that authority as the amount fairly chargeable in the case.*

Now, through the operation of a monetary system established and kept in existence by the State, the amounts thus legally chargeable have come to represent obligations vastly more burdensome than those

---

[1] See pages 43; 48-50; 52, 53.

originally imposed. Surely, then, it is but a manifest requirement of equity, that, in view of the unforeseen additional burden which now has to be borne, the terms of payment should, as speedily as possible, be readjusted by that same public authority by which they were originally fixed.

It comes, then, to this.

If the State is unable or unwilling to apply a radical remedy, by boldly reforming its currency arrangements out of which the existing evil has grown, it surely is bound to take in hand the readjustment of the terms of those obligations which, through the working of those currency arrangements, have grown to be so oppressively burdensome.

It is said that, from the overpowering influence of the capitalists, the money-owners and money-lenders, of the world, it is futile to expect that the evils resulting from the operation of the present system of currency shall be boldly grappled with in their root.

Whether this is so or not, I have no means of knowing.

The question I have to put is whether, in view of the facts to which I call attention in this Pamphlet, there can be any room for doubt that it is the plain duty of the public authority of the country to take some effective steps, whatever they may be, to hinder the tenants and tenant-purchasers of Ireland from being dragged down gradually to hopeless ruin?

✠ W. J. W.

Archbishop's House,
Dublin, 10th *February*, 1893.

INTERVIEW.

[Republished, with numerous additions and illustrative notes, from the *Freeman's Journal and National Press* (Dublin) of Monday, November 28th, 1892.]

WE have the permission of the Archbishop of Dublin to publish the following important Interview in reference to an incident of his Grace's examination before the Evicted Tenants' Commission last Thursday.[1]

The Interview, as will be seen, has reference primarily to the equitableness of certain terms of settlement which were proposed by the landlord at a critical stage of the dispute on the Coolgreany estate, in the County of Wicklow and Diocese of Dublin.

The Archbishop had made more than one effort to bring about a settlement of the dispute between landlord and tenants on that estate by means of arbitration—the award of the arbitrators, as suggested by his Grace, to be based upon the decisions of the Courts of the Land Commission. The landlord, however, was inflexible in his refusal to accept the decisions of the Courts as an admissible basis of settlement. In October, 1887, then, he proposed certain terms of his own, which the tenants could not see their way to agree to.

An important portion of the Archbishop's examination before the Evicted Tenants' Commission had reference to the terms so proposed by the landlord, and to the tenants' rejection of them. His Grace explained that, whilst he had

---

[1] See the *Freeman's Journal and National Press* (Dublin) of Friday, Nov. 25th, 1892.

in no way interfered in reference to the acceptance or rejection of the terms in question, he was not at all surprised when he heard of the decision that was come to by the tenants not to accept them.

They were, the Archbishop said, "attractive-looking proposals." The reduction to the tenants, in which they would result, was a reduction of 36 per cent, whilst the tenants' original claim, about which they had got into cross-purposes with the landlord, was for a reduction only of 30 per cent.

But, as his Grace pointed out, there is an element in the case, which it is of essential importance to take into account in any comparison between the rate of reduction involved in the terms proposed by the landlord, and that pressed for in the tenants' claim.

The point is fully brought out in the following extract from the Archbishop's examination before the Commission :

" *Mr. Redington*—Why should they [the Coolgreany tenants] get more reduction than a fair rent ?

" *The Archbishop*—A reduction [such as was proposed by the landlord] would not give them a fair rent. . . . A 36 per cent reduction might have given them a fair rent for that year. But there is this to be considered. A fair rent, provided it is not a 'judicial rent' [under the Land Act of 1881], can be revised from year to year : the great majority of Irish landlords are quite willing to make reasonable reductions in bad years. So then, a fair rent from year to year is one thing : a 'judicial' rent is very different ; if there is a 'judicial' rent, it will stand for 15 years. That makes a notable difference. But then, under this arrangement [proposed to the Coolgreany tenants by the landlord], the effect of the contract was to last, not merely for 15 years, but for

49 years [inasmuch as the acceptance of the proposed term by the tenants would involve their becoming tenant-purchasers under the Land Purchase Act, and so placing themselves under an obligation of paying a fixed amount to the Government for 49 years] ; and that might be ruinous to the tenants.

" *Mr. Redington*—You say it might not be ruinous if fixed for 15 years, but that it might be if fixed for 49 or 50 years ?

" *The Archbishop*—Yes.

" *Sir Jas. Mathew*—Did you say 15 years ?

" *The Archbishop*—I said it might be perfectly reasonable for one year ; for, if the next year happened to be a bad year, then there could be a revision of the terms. But going under a fixed rent for 15 years is a very different thing. A tenant runs a heavy risk if he pledges himself to pay any fixed sum of money for 15 years. But then, if he has to pledge himself to pay a fixed sum for so long a period as 49 or 50 years, he runs a serious risk, indeed, of ending in bankruptcy. I speak in view of the present state of affairs in the world of money.

*　　　○　　　*

" *Mr. Redington*—You think that in the case of 50 years, the reduction should be greater ?

" *The Archbishop*—Yes. May I explain my reason ? If so, I would give you an extract from a speech of Mr. Balfour's—it is not contentious—

" *Sir Jas. Mathew*—No, no.

" *The Archbishop* (handing a pamphlet to the President, which Sir James accepted)—There really is nothing contentious in it. Mr. Balfour in this speech[1] lays down the proposition that the difficulty of paying any fixed

---

[1] See pages 52 , 53.

amount of money is increasing from year to year. That is my reason for saying that it would be a very serious risk for a tenant to expose himself to, if he were to enter into a contract to pay a fixed sum for 49 years."

Our representative explained to the Archbishop that a good deal of curiosity and of interest has been felt in reference to this incident of his Grace's examination.

"As to discussing anything that occurred at the Commission," said the Archbishop, "I must at once say that I cannot comply with your request. The wish of the Commissioners that comments should not be made seems to be very generally respected in the newspapers all round. This is as it should be. I can have nothing to do with anything that might tend to encroach upon this principle of reserve.

"Personally, indeed, I see a very strong reason in favour of the view taken by Sir James Mathew in this matter. There is no reason why I should not now say to you that the point I thought of referring to was one which, no doubt, will seem to you, as it must seem to most people, to lie very far off, indeed, from the Irish Land Question. It was that perplexing subject—as so many regard it—which is known as Bimetallism.

"You will understand, of course, that in calling Bimetallism a perplexing topic, I am speaking of Bimetallism only as it is commonly spoken of. In reality there is nothing perplexing about it. Many people, however, seem to think that there is. But, at all events, whether the subject is a perplexing one or not, there is a prejudice against Bimetallism—a prejudice, especially, on the part of the capitalists, the money-owning, and, most especially, the money-lending, classes of the world.[1]

" This, then, is why I say that I see a strong reason for the view taken by the President of the Evicted Tenants Commission in refusing to admit any reference to that financial topic. In the minds of large numbers of more or less influential people, a somewhat serious obstacle might have been put in the way of an unprejudiced consideration of the case of the evicted tenants, if it came to be supposed that the view to be taken of the case of those tenants was in any way dependent upon the adoption either of Bimetallism or of the opposite theory of Monometallism.

" The case of the evicted tenants is already quite complicated enough. It would be unwise to complicate it still further by even seeming to make the solution of the difficulty depend upon the view to be taken of any of the points at issue between the Bimetallists and their Monometallist opponents.

" But now my view of the case of the evicted tenants, as I put it before the Commission, stands quite clear of any difficulty which a reference to Bimetallism might have raised. This point being secured, I have no objection whatever to say to you everything I have to say upon the subject of Bimetallism in its bearing upon our present system of Land Tenure in Ireland."

" The connection, your Grace, between Bimetallism and the Irish Land Question does not seem very close ? "

" Yet nothing could be closer. The adoption of

---

[1] See pages 43 : 48-50 ; 52, 53.

Bimetallism, or of some equivalent remedy, if there be
an equivalent remedy, is, I am convinced, a matter of
imperative necessity ; that is, if the agricultural tenants of
Ireland—and I do not at all limit this to Ireland—are to
be saved from otherwise inevitable ruin.

" This is transparently obvious to everyone who has
mastered even the elementary facts and principles of the
case. But it is disheartening to find that, notwithstanding
all this, no interest seems to be taken in this grave
question by many of the leaders of Irish opinion.

" If things go on as they are, even the excellent Land
Purchase scheme which is associated with the name of
Lord Ashbourne may become, before many years are over,
a source of widespread disaster to the tenants who have
purchased under it."

" But no one seems to be aware of this ? "

" On the contrary, it is thoroughly well known to every
Bimetallist.

" The Monometallists also — at all events very
many of them, and, amongst these, some of the more
prominent champions of their cause—fully recognise the
truth of it. But as there is some difference of opinion
about it amongst Monometallists, and as it certainly is
not involved in any of the distinctive principles of their
theory, I prefer to reserve for a little what I have to say
about the support, the strong support, which even the very
gloomiest view of the prospects of our Irish farmers receives
from the Monometallist side.[1]

" The great point of difference between Bimetallists and
Monometallists in such a case as this, is, that the Mono-

[1] See pages 56-71.

metallists have no practical remedy to propose, whilst the Bimetallists have.[1] The principle of the Monometallists seems to be the old *laissez-faire* principle,—that things must become a great deal worse before they can be any better. At all events they have no practical remedy to propose. The Bimetallists have. But, unhappily, the Bimetallists cannot get anyone in Ireland to listen to them. So far as I can see, the case, in this aspect of it, is all but hopeless.

"By those who know nothing about this question—and, of course, they are the great majority—Bimetallism is set down as a sort of craze, and a craze harmless only in the sense that, as is foolishly thought, a dispute about systems of currency can have no bearing upon any practical affair of life. This is a very common view. What possible chance, then, is there of stirring up public opinion upon the question? Efforts in that direction have already been made. They are fruitless. How many people in Ireland know, for instance, that an admirable little pamphlet has been published upon this question by one of the ablest of our Irish members of Parliament, Mr. Knox,[2] the Member for Cavan ? "

"Mr. Knox, then, recognises that there is a connection between the controversy about Bimetallism and the Irish Land Question ? "

"Of course he does. To everyone who knows anything even of the elements of this question, the connection between Bimetallism and the Irish Land Question is so obvious that the fact of its not being grasped by every man of intelligence is simply inexplicable.

[1] See page 87-96.
[2] *The Irish Land Question as affected by the Appreciation of Gold.* By E. F. Vesey Knox. M.P.: Dublin, London, and Manchester, 1892.

"The subject of Mr. Knox's pamphlet is, the Irish Land Question as affected by the difficulties that result from our monetary system no longer standing upon a Bimetallic footing. 'As probably everyone in Ireland,' he says, 'except the gombeen man,[1] is a loser by the present monetary system, it seems strange that so little attention has been called to the Irish aspects of the Bimetallic controversy.'

"What those aspects are, Mr. Knox puts very plainly. Here is how he states the case :—

"'We have a tenantry owning a sort of half property in the soil, and their general relations with their landlords are such that a readjustment [of rent] by agreement seems impossible.

"'To meet this difficulty, two steps have been taken by the State. In the first place, rents are fixed by the Land Commission for the term of 15 years. In the second place, money is lent to the tenants by the State for the purchase of their holdings, on terms which usually give a material reduction of annual payment, but make that annual payment a fixed quantity for 50 years. . .

"'The tenant under a 'judicial term' finds that, though his rent is nominally a fixed quantity for 15 years, it is really rising.'

"That is to say, the rent is rising, in the sense that, year after year, it is becoming *more and more difficult for the tenant to pay that fixed rent out of the product of his industry.*

"Then, as to those who have purchased under the Ashbourne Purchase Act, Mr. Knox continues :—'The purchaser under the Ashbourne Act may not have felt the pressure as yet ; but as years go on . . . he will find it

---

[1] A popular designation in Ireland for the money-lenders, especially for those of the rural districts, the villages, and the smaller towns.

increasingly difficult to pay the same sum as heretofore to the State.'"

" The subject of Bimetallism is at all events an exceedingly obscure one ?"

"Not at all. There is, no doubt, even amongst eminent financial authorities, a difference of opinion whether the Bimetallist view as to the direction in which a remedy for the existing state of depression should be sought for, is the true view of the case or not. But Bimetallism is in no sense an obscure subject. There is no difficulty whatever in understanding it—no difficulty in understanding either what it is in itself, or how it bears upon the Irish Land Question."

The Archbishop then, in compliance with a request that he would indicate at least the general outlines of the subject, remarked that it was a subject impossible to deal with in any way that could be called brief.

"Bimetallism," he said, "embraces, no doubt, some points that may be omitted in a merely summary exposition of it—especially in a statement of those aspects of it that have special reference to the Irish Land Question. But in any case a good deal must remain to be said.

" As for the Irish farmers, it is to be remembered that the way they come into consideration in the matter is this: —Our farmers, many of them, are placed under an obligation to pay, annually, a fixed amount of money—'fixed,' that is to say, in the sense that the amount they have to pay, year after year, for a prolonged term of years, is specified in pounds, shillings, and pence.

" There are three classes of our Irish farmers lying

under such an obligation. In the first place, some have, as ordinary leaseholders, to pay, for longer or shorter periods, a sum so fixed. Others have to pay a fixed sum for 15 years, as 'judicial' tenants under the arrangements of the Land Act of 1881. Others,—as tenant-purchasers under one or other of the Irish Land Purchase Acts,—have to pay, for 49 years, a fixed sum to the Government.

" Now, in the present condition of our currency laws, any obligation of paying a fixed amount of money for a prolonged term of years may bring with it financial ruin to the unfortunate tenant who has undertaken that obligation, or upon whom it has been imposed by law.

" Indeed I may say that, under the operation of the present Monometallic system of currency, any such obligation must, in the course of time, bring with it, if not financial ruin, at all events most serious financial embarrassment. The reason is obvious. The conditions of the case are such that, notwithstanding the so-called 'fixing' of the amount to be paid each year, the payment of the amount thus 'fixed' in pounds, shillings, and pence, *really represents a burden growing heavier and heavier from year to year.*

" This is how the tenants' case stands, in the view, at all events, of the Bimetallists—to say nothing, for the present, about the extent to which, upon this particular point, the views of the Bimetallists are shared by some leading upholders of Monometallism.[1] As for the Bimetallists, it is important to remember, especially upon a point such as this, that one of the leading champions of Bimetallism, is Mr. Balfour, our late Chief Secretary for Ireland.[2]

" With Mr. Balfour, then, as with all Bimetallists, it is a

[1] See page 6.   [2] See pages 52, 53.

cardinal principle that, as a direct result of the present monetary system of England and of other leading commercial European countries, everyone who is under an obligation to make a yearly or other periodic payment of a 'fixed' amount,—as, for instance, a 'judicial' tenant under the Land Act of 1881, or an Irish tenant-purchaser under the Ashbourne Act of 1885 or any subsequent enactment,—is thereby *placed under a burden which necessarily grows heavier from year to year.*

"All this, the Bimetallists make good in proof. But, quite apart from the proofs which they bring forward, can anyone deny that even the mere authority of so many men of eminence in financial science as are to be found in the ranks of the Bimetallists ought to count for a good deal? It surely should suffice, at the very least, to show that any one—any tenant, for instance —will have only himself to blame for whatever disaster may befal him if, he disregards the clear and impressive warning given him by Mr. Balfour and other Bimetallists of the gulf that is yawning before him, and takes upon himself an obligation to pay yearly, for 49 years, or even for 15 years, a 'fixed' amount of money,—that is to say, an amount specified in pounds, shillings, and pence,—without making full allowance in his calculations for the risk he runs of finding himself, as years go on, overloaded, and, in the end crushed, by the weight of an ever-increasing burden.

"The Bimetallists may be right or they may be wrong. But, at all events, if they are right, then it is undisputably plain that the Irish tenants who have the misfortune to have their rents fixed for terms of 15 years, under the Land Act of 1881,—and, much more so, the Irish tenant-purchasers, who have the misfortune to find themselves saddled with the obligation of making annual payments fixed for 49 years,—are simply slipping down an inclined plane, with bankruptcy awaiting them at the bottom of it.

"It is only quite recently that I came to know something of the gravity of the present state of affairs. Now that I have become aware of it, I feel bound, as a matter of public duty, to do what I can to bring it to the knowledge of those whom it most concerns.

"In connection with all this, I would again call attention to the fact that, in such a case, Mr. Balfour's authority[1] must be recognised as of exceptional weight. Surely the tenants, and those who advocate or represent the tenants' views, ought to insist that this point, which is brought out so forcibly by Mr. Balfour and others, shall be taken into account as an important element in the fixing of fair rents for terms of years, and—as a matter of still higher importance—in the fixing of terms of purchase involving the obligation of fixed annual payments for still longer periods. The point, as I have already stated it, is, that *everyone who is placed under an obligation to make yearly payments of a fixed amount of money, is thereby placed under a burden which is growing heavier from year to year.*

"If this point be insisted upon, as assuredly it ought to be, by the tenants and by their representatives and advocates, how can the landlords, or those who advocate and represent the views of the landlords, take it upon themselves to say that the Bimetallists are not to be listened to in the case? Their ideal statesman, Mr. Balfour, they must be reminded, is a pronounced and thorough-going Bimetallist. From this point of view, the emphatic

[1] See pages 52, 53.

and unqualified declaration of our late Chief Secretary is of momentous importance.

" Then, if anything more is wished for than the mere authority of the Bimetallists—more even than the authority of Mr. Balfour himself—let me point out how their conclusion is reached.

" I happen to have here a Statement which I wrote, for another purpose, some time ago, and which I can give to you. It is a statement of a few elementary facts and principles of political economy—facts and principles that must underlie every explanation of the currency question. The points set out in it are purely elementary matters. They require, I think, no explanation, as they certainly require no proof.

" They are these [1]:—

" 1. Money forms our common medium of exchange. At first, commerce, such as it was, had to be carried on by a system of pure barter—the system in which, for instance, so many sheep were given in exchange for so many cows, so much corn for so much wool, and so on. Then, as civilization progressed, this system of pure barter was displaced by the employment of a common medium of exchange, available in all cases of selling and buying. Great diversity existed among various tribes and peoples in the choice of the particular medium employed. In some places, skins were used; in some, leather ; in some, corn ; in some, cattle. Then came a higher stage of development, when metals, such as iron, tin, lead, and copper, were employed. But now, with practical universality, all other

---

[1] Only five of the points contained in this Statement were stated in the original Interview.

materials for standard money have given place to gold and silver.[1]

"2. 'Money, as regards its primary function, is simply a commodity, selected first by custom, and (often, but not always) confirmed by law, as an intermediary in transactions—a something for which, in a civilized community, any other thing can be sold, and with which any other thing can be bought. In other words, a particular commodity is selected to perform the function of a common measure of value; but it is, and remains, a commodity. Gold remains gold, silver remains silver, while they perform this function of money; and they remain subject to exactly the same laws of exchange as before. A new use is imposed upon the substance; that is all; the substance itself is unchanged.'[2]

"3. By the 'value' of money, we are to understand its 'exchange value,' or, in other words, its purchasing power—that is to say, the power which the possession of money gives to those who possess it, to go into an open market, and obtain, in exchange for their money, the things that are on sale there.

"4. The metals, gold and silver, like all other marketable commodities, are liable to fluctuations in value; their value being controlled, like that of all other commodities, by the law of supply and demand.[3] This means that if gold

---

[1] See Professor Nicholson's Treatise or. *Money and Monetary Problems:* Edinburgh and London, 1888. pp. 38, 39.

[2] *The Case against Bimetallism.* By Robert Giffen: London, 1892, pages 194, 5. Mr. Giffen, in his Introduction, apologises for inserting elementary matter about the nature of Money in a book on Bimetallism. "Bimetallists," he says, "in fact have made it necessary for us to go back to first principles, to begin at the beginning" (*Ibid.* p. 7). The drift of this remark is not very obvious. There is nothing in the passage above quoted which Bimetallists can have the slightest difficulty in accepting as a matter of fundamental principle. (See also pages 84-86 of this Pamphlet.)

[3] "Economists justly assert that while metallic money is a standard of value in relation to other commodities, it is also itself a commodity, and, as

and silver are to be had in abundance, a smaller quantity of other commodities— as, for instance, less corn, less hay, less butter—will have to be given in exchange for a definite quantity of gold and silver. On the other hand, if gold and silver are not so easily to be had, then, a larger quantity of other commodities,—more corn, for instance, more hay, more butter—will have to be parted with, to obtain in exchange for them the same quantity of those metals.

"5 . ' It is now universally admitted in works of Political Economy that any such thing as a commodity with absolute stability of value is unattainable.' [1]

" 6. 'The most important characteristic of a good monetary standard is, that it should preserve comparative stability of value. The principal reason why, of the multitude of commodities that have been used for the material of money at different times, gold and silver have survived as the fittest, is because their great durability renders the total stock extremely large compared with the annual supply, and thus eliminates one element of instability of value.' [2]

" 7. Another special advantage of gold and silver for monetary purposes is that both the weight and the purity of coins made from them may easily be ascertained. 'At first, after gold and silver were generally adopted, the risk of being defrauded by inferior quality or adulteration was left entirely to the receivers of the metals ; in fact, gold and silver circulated between the inhabitants

such, is subject to the laws which rule the value of all other commodities. Scarcity must enhance its value, and abundance must diminish its value." *The Silver Question and the Gold Question.* By Robert Barclay (3rd Edition) : Manchester and London, page 24.

[1] *Money and Monetary Problems.* By J. Shield Nicholson ; Edinburgh and London, 1888. Page 25.

[2] *Ibid.*, pages 281, 2.

of the country simply as merchandise. . . . Very early, however, it began to be recognised that there would be great convenience if pieces of the metal were certified by authority to be of certain weights and fineness; and, accordingly, coinage has always been one of the first industrial functions that governments have undertaken.'[1]

"8. Coinage is only a process of branding or stamping, and nothing else. The process of minting certifies two things: first, that the coin is of a certain weight of gold or silver, as the case may be; and, secondly that the gold or silver of which the coin is composed is of a certain specified degree of purity.[2] But minting—the minting, for instance, of gold into a sovereign—adds nothing to the value of the piece of metal that is coined.

"9. It is not, however, to be supposed that the commodity, gold, or the commodity, silver, does not derive a special value from the fact of its being constituted a standard monetary metal. 'Law singles out gold or silver, or both, to be used as money, and gives them special functions which it confers on no other commodity. *In*

[1] Nicholson, *Money and Monetary Problems,* pp. 42, 43,

[2] This, of course, applies only to the "standard" coinage of a country. "In every country, every coin must be referred to the standard if we are to know their value. Thus, *a shilling means the twentieth part of a sovereign*. . .

"The relation which a coin professes to bear to the standard is called the *denomination* of the coin. Hence an important distinction of two kinds of coin : standard and token coins

"*Standard coins* are those whose denomination is really in accord with their material and weight. Thus among ourselves a well-preserved sovereign and half-sovereign are standard coins. They profess to be, respectively, one, and one-half, of the standard unit of value ; and they are.

"*Token coins* are those whose denomination is not really in accord with their material and weight ; they are lacking in fineness or weight, or both, and they may even be of another metal than the standard. Nevertheless their exchange value may keep as high as their denomination, because they can be exchanged at law for what they are . . . Thus *the denomination of our English shilling is the twentieth part of a sovereign,* and twenty shillings will buy exactly as much as one sovereign, though the metal in them is really worth only three-quarters of a sovereign, if as much." *Political Economy.* By Charles S. Devas : London, 1892, pages 267, 8.

virtue of this selection, the demand for these metals is greatly increased, and, as they are only of limited production, *their value is increased accordingly*' [1]

" 10. A sovereign is a minted coin consisting of a certain specified weight of gold, of a certain specified fineness. The weight of a sovereign when issued from the Mint is the $\frac{160}{623}$rd part of an ounce, or 123·27447 grains, of standard gold.[2]

" 11. A fluctuation in the value of gold involves a fluctuation in the value of the sovereign.

"This, of course, does not mean that the sovereign

---

[1] *The Silver Question and the Gold Question.* By Robert Barclay (3rd Edition) : Manchester and London ; page 45.
Or as Mr. Samuel Smith expresses it, though possibly in a somewhat exaggerated form :—
" Gold and Silver derive their value mainly from their use as money . . If all the world passed such laws as England and Germany have done [allowing Silver to be coined only in limited quantity, and not recognising it, except in cases of small payments, as legal tender], Silver would be almost valueless.
" At least £500,000,000 sterling of that metal, now circulating [in certain countries] as full legal tender, would be expelled, and, as not a hundredth part of it would be wanted for plate and ornaments, it would have to be degraded to some mechanical use, where it would compete with iron and steel, and be sold by the ton, instead of by the ounce." *The Bimetallic Question.* By Samuel Smith, M.P., London, 1887. (Essay on *Bimetallic Money*, page 22).
[2] The gold in a sovereign is not absolutely pure. Pure gold is too soft for use in coins. The Coinage Act of 1870—in substance the same as that of 1816,—fixes both the weight of the sovereign and the proportion of alloy. The proportion is, 1 part of copper with 11 of pure gold. Gold of this degree of fineness is technically described as " 22 carat " gold, there being 22 parts of pure gold in every 24.
As regards the mintage of gold, anyone can take any quantity of standard (22 carat) gold to the Mint, and get it coined into sovereigns or half-sovereigns free of charge : 160 ounces of gold being coined into 623 sovereigns. What is known as " the mint price of gold," £3 17s. 10½d., per ounce—this being at the rate of 623 sovereigns for 160 ounces—simply indicates the number of standard coins that will be made at the Mint out of a certain amount of standard metal. In other words a Troy ounce of standard gold is coined into 3.89375 sovereigns.
"Practically, the time and trouble involved in going direct to the Mint induced people to sell their gold direct to the Bank of England. The Bank is compelled to purchase all standard gold at £3 17s. 9d. per ounce, and, as it obtains from the Mint £3 17s. 10½d., there is a small profit by way of brokerage."—*Chambers's Encyclopædia* (new edition) ; London and Edinburgh, 1891, vol. vii., page 270.

can ever become worth more or less than twenty shillings. That would be a contradiction in terms. For, 'a shilling' means merely the twentieth part of the value of a sovereign.[1]

"When we say, then, that the value of a sovereign may fluctuate, what we mean is that, as a medium of exchange, the sovereign will sometimes have a greater, sometimes a lesser, 'exchange value' or purchasing power.[2]

"The reason of the liability to fluctuation in the purchasing power of the sovereign is plain. When gold rises in value, a larger quantity of any other commodity,—say, of corn, of hay, of butter, or of cloth, —will have to be given in exchange for any given quantity of gold, such, for example, as the quantity contained in a sovereign. On the other hand, when gold falls in value, a smaller quantity of any other commodity,—say, of corn, of hay, of butter, or of cloth,—will suffice to obtain in exchange for it any given quantity of gold, such as that contained in a sovereign.

" 12. It is an obvious inference, that our gold coinage, however useful as a medium of exchange, does not furnish us with a standard of value, fixed and unalterable. It does not furnish us, for example, with such a standard as the yard is of length, or as the pound Troy is of weight.

---

[1] See page 16. *footnote* 2.

[2] See pages 14, 15.

[3] " It may seem at first sight almost contradictory to speak of variations in the value of the monetary standard. How, it may be asked, can the standard, which is the measure of value, itself vary in value?

" At present in this country, the sovereign is apparently the standard measure of value, just as the yard is the standard measure of length ; and it would certainly seem odd to most people to speak even hypothetically of variations in the measuring power of the standard yard.

" It may be useful, for purposes of comparison and contrast, to quote the definitions of the standard yard and of the sovereign or pound sterling.

" By Act of Parliament, 30th July, 1855, it was enacted :—' That the straight line or distance between the centres of the transverse lines in the two gold plugs in the bronze bar deposited in the office of the Exchequer, shall be the genuine standard yard, at 62° Fahrenheit.'

" According to the Coinage Act, renewed in 1870, the sovereign is defined as consisting of 123·27447 grains of English standard gold . .

" When we compare the two definitions, we see that whilst the former

" 13. The popular notion, then, of the sovereign, or pound sterling, constituting a fixed standard of value, is merely a popular delusion.

"The sole foundation for that delusion manifestly is, that, in these countries, the values of all commodities are commonly stated in terms of the pound sterling, in other words, in pounds, shillings and pence,—'a shilling' meaning the twentieth part of a pound, and 'a penny,' the twelfth part of that again. The natural result of this method of expressing the values of commodities other than gold, is, that, to the superficial observer, the impression conveyed by a rise or fall in prices is that it is the value of all other things that changes, the value of the sovereign remaining fixed.

" 14. In Great Britain,—and the same is true of Ireland, and of many other countries—gold being the one standard metal, all prices are stated in terms of the sovereign, or of parts of the sovereign. So that for instance, if, at any time, a certain quantity of corn sells for £100 5s. 10d., this means that this quantity of corn represents, in exchange-value, 100 sovereigns, with the fourth part (5s.) of the value of a sovereign, and the sixth part (10d.) of that again.

refers definitely to the distance between two points, or to length, the latter refers only to *the weight of a particular substance*, and *says nothing of value.*

" In the definition of a standard yard, a definite place and a definite temperature are mentioned, and other precautions are implied, which render the standard for practical purposes invariable, In the definition of the sovereign, also, similarly precise elements are found ; but *they refer only to weight and chemical composition, not to value.*

"Strictly speaking, then, it is only by accident that the sovereign can ever be a standard of value at different times and places, in the same way as the yard is the standard of length.

"Acres, bushels, tons, have a precise meaning as regards extension. capacity, and weight, but *the pound sterling* has *no precise meaning as regards value.* . .

" A *certain weight of standard gold* is a very different thing from a *certain amount of purchasing power.*" Nicholson's *Money and Monetary Problems*, pages 298-303

" But in countries, such as India, where silver is the one standard metal, all prices are stated in reference to the rupee,—a standard silver coin which may be compared, roughly, with our two-shilling piece.

" Prices stated in terms of a standard gold coin, as they are stated in England and Ireland in terms of the sovereign, are spoken of as ' gold ' prices.   Prices stated in terms of a standard silver coin, as they are stated in India in terms of the rupee, are spoken of as ' silver ' prices.

" 15. The price of things estimated in gold,—their ' gold price '—may change, whilst their price estimated in silver— their ' silver price '—remains unaltered.'

" This will occur if the value or purchasing power of gold goes up or down, while the value or purchasing power of silver remains unaltered.

" Suppose, for instance, that gold is in any way scarce in relation to the demand upon it.   Then in any country where gold is the standard metal of the currency, those who wish to obtain a certain quantity of gold, whether in coin or in bullion, will have to give a larger quantity of other commodities in exchange for it, or—to put the

---

[1] " In order to avoid a common source of confusion, it may be well to explain that [what we here speak of is] the determination of *general* prices, and not . . the changes in the *relative* values of commodities . . .

" It is easy to see how, from causes affecting some particular article, that article may have fallen or risen in value; and similarly, through the whole range of commodities, we may discover causes which have made some to rise and others to fall.

" If, however, we find that, apart from these *relative* changes, *a general change in the level* [of prices] has occurred, it is natural to conclude that this is due either to *causes primarily affecting the standard by which prices are determined*, or to causes of a very wide-reaching character affecting commodities.

" It cannot be too often insisted on that the real meaning of the value of money is *its value compared with things in general*—that is, its value as determined by *the general level of prices*." Nicholson, *Money and Monetary Problems*, page 63.

" ' Things in general ' is, of course, a vague and rather uncertain expression, but it is perhaps the best obtainable." *Ibid.* page 30.

As to all this, see pages 58-64 of this Pamphlet.

matter in another light—those who have only a definite quantity of commodities to part with will receive less gold in return for them. In other words, there is a fall in 'gold prices.'

"Suppose, on the contrary, that gold is abundant in relation to the demand upon it. Then those who wish to obtain a certain quantity of gold, whether in coin or in bullion, will not have to give so large a quantity of other commodities to obtain the quantity of gold they require, or—to put the matter, as before, in another light—those who have a definite quantity of other commodities to dispose of will obtain more gold in return for them. In other words, there is a rise in 'gold prices.'

"If, in either case, there is no change in the value of silver, then the prices of commodities, stated in silver—their 'silver prices,' as the technical phrase is—will remain unchanged.

"Similarly, of course, the 'silver price' of things may change, while their 'gold price' remains unaltered."

"Is this common ground, so far?"

"Yes. But now we reach the point at which Monometallists and Bimetallists begin to differ. Take it in this way. A country may arrange its system of standard money upon either of two bases: it may take only one of the precious metals as its standard of value——"

"This is Monometallism?"

"Yes; no matter whether the metal selected is gold or silver.

"India, for instance, is a 'silver' monometallic country: the standard there is a rupee—a silver coin, which, as I have already said, may be compared, roughly, with our florin or two-shilling piece.

"England, on the other hand, is a 'gold' monometallic country, the standard coin being the sovereign. As to the silver coins of the English currency, every one knows that, though they are current in a certain limited quantity, they are not 'legal tender' in payment of debts for any amount beyond 40s.[1] The silver coins, then, of the English mint are merely what are termed 'token coins,'—the value of the silver in twenty of our shilling-pieces being altogether short of the value of the gold in a sovereign." [2]

"Then as to Bimetallism?"

"Bimetallism, as some writers express it, is the monetary system in which the two precious metals, gold and silver, are taken as standards of currency.

"That, however, is a misleading way of putting the

---

[1] "*Money* is any exchangeable good which is both a medium of exchange and a measure of exchange-value.

"*Currency* is any medium of exchange which is current in a certain region, that is to say, which freely circulates there—which as a rule every one there will take in exchange.

"*Legal Tender* is any medium of exchange which every one must by law take in exchange unless he has previously made a special arrangement to the contrary with the other party to any contract.

"According to these definitions the bank-notes of a local banker in an English country town are Currency, for every one there will take them ; but they are not Legal Tender or real Money.

"In the same town, a note of the Bank of England is both Currency and Legal Tender, for if a man owes me five pounds I cannot refuse such a note in payment ; but such a note is not real Money, for it does not serve as a real measure of exchange-value.

"Lastly, in the same town, a gold sovereign is both Currency, and Legal Tender, and real Money."

"According also to these definitions we must never use the phrase 'paper money,' which is almost a contradiction in terms. Promises are not the same as performance, and the proper phrase is *paper currency* : and if we are bent on applying the word Money to paper, at least let us always add that it is only nominal not real money." *Political Economy.* By Charles S. Devas : London 1892, pages 252, 3.

[2] See page 16. *footnote* 2.

case. The word Bimetallism indeed is an unfortunate one to have been chosen. It gives prominence to the idea of duality, and so leads many half-informed people to think that Bimetallism, as distinct from Monometallism, aims at having two standards of value, instead of one.

"Now this is not at all the case. In the Bimetallist system there are not two standards of value; there is but one.[1] One of the essential requirements of a standard, whether of value, or of length, or of weight, or of anything else, is that it should be one. The word Bimetallism, then, as I have said, is, in one respect, an unfortunate one to have been chosen. It gives rise to an unhappy notion that the Bimetallists favour some sort of shifting or alternative system of standards. But this is not so. The very opposite is the fact. Unity of standard and stability of standard—in so far as stability in this matter of a standard of value is within the reach of attainment[2]— these are the very fundamental points of Bimetallism."

"Is not this so also in Monometallism?"

"No. A little further on we shall deal with the important point of stability in the standard of value.[3] But take first this matter of unity of standard. Does Monometallism secure unity? Nothing of the kind. What have we,

---

[1] " The central idea of what is known as the Bimetallic movement is to restore the unity of money ; to re-establish unity between the two centres of valuation— the gold valuation and the silver valuation -so that they may again do their work in harmony.

" Unfortunately, the name ' Bimetallic ' does not clearly convey this idea, and instead of seeking restoration and unity, the movement is too often supposed to be one for the initiation of something new, and an attempt to create an impossible duality." *The Silver Question and the Gold Question.* By Robert Barclay (Third Edition) : Manchester and London. Page 104.

[2] See page 15. [3] See pages 45 ; 91, 92.

as the result of the present predominance of Monometal-lism in so many countries? Simply division and confusion.[1]

"In one set of countries, such as England and Ireland, gold is the standard metal. In another set of countries, such as India, the standard is silver.[2] When a 'silver' country, such as India, comes to trade with a 'gold' country, such as England, see what happens. Gold and silver are two independent commodities. In the markets of the world, then, each, from the operation of the law of supply and demand, is subject to its own independent fluctuations in value.[3] There is nothing to keep the relative values of the two at a fixed ratio to one another. So, the 'gold price' of silver, or, in other words, the 'silver price' of gold, is constantly changing.[4]

"Take the last 19 or 20 years, for instance. The 'gold price' of silver per ounce has ranged from 5s. 0d. down to 3s. 3d. This necessarily has affected the relative

---

[1] "In seeking unity of standard in one metal, the Monometallic school has, in effect, brought about the destruction of the unity of money.

"It ignored the actual conditions of money throughout the world, and overlooked the interdependence which must necessarily exist between the gold money and the silver money of the world. These form in their aggregate, whether working together or separately, the basis of monetary valuation. . .

"Here, then, is the true position of this monetary question. The Mono-metallist is the partisan of a school of innovators whose idea of setting up a standard of value in one metal which would be a true measure of value has lamentably failed, and has resulted in the monetary confusion which we see to-day. The Bimetallist, on the other hand, seeks to arrest this confusion by returning to the old paths, and restoring the unity of money by linking gold and silver together and making them virtually one by the tie of a fixed ratio." *The Silver Question and the Gold Question.* By Robert Barclay. Third Edition. Pages 106-7.

[2] "The British Empire is neither Monometallist nor Bimetallist, but *Bi-monometallist.*

"The British Empire cannot be Monometallist gold, nor Monometallist silver, throughout its length and breadth,

"Its present position of Bi-monometallism is entirely inconsistent. . . . It cannot maintain the permanent position of a house divided against itself which cannot stand." Mr. Ewarts, Secretary of State. U.S.A, (quoted in *Silver and Gold; the Money of the World,* by Sir Guilford L. Molesworth : London and Manchester, 1891. Page 39.)

[3] See pages 14, 15.
[4] See pages 20, 21.

value of gold and silver coins.[1] The Indian rupee, then, which formerly counted as a two-shilling piece— 10 rupees being, roughly, the equivalent in value of a sovereign—came tumbling down in value until, as measured by the sovereign, it was worth only 1s. 3d. or 1s. 4d.

"In other words, a person in India, who, for any purpose, had to make a remittance of £50 to England, would some years ago have found 500 rupees sufficient, but of late years he might have had to send 800."[2]

"This is from a fall in the value of silver?"

"It could happen as the result either of a fall in the value of silver, or of a rise in the value of gold.

"So far as the facts I have as yet stated are concerned, the change in the relative values of the sovereign and the rupee may have come either from one cause or from the other. We shall afterwards deal with the cause of the change.[3] I am now merely calling attention to the fact that, as things are, we have, under the denomination of so-called Monometallism, not one common standard of value, but two distinct standards—gold, in England, for instance, and silver in India—each metal being liable to fluctuation in value, and the fluctuations in one being wholly independent

---

[1] See pages 17 and 18.

[2] "The Indian Government engages the services of a highly trained body of men, and promises to pay them a certain number of rupees.

"There is no doubt as to the meaning of the rupee in its material shape. It is *a certain weight of a certain quantity of silver*.

"Suppose at the time the bargain is made, 10 rupees go to a sovereign, then the savings of Indian officials remitted home [to England] will command that rate as long as it lasts. But it is equally clear that if [from a change in the relative values of gold and silver] the value of the rupee sinks to a shilling [that is, to the twentieth part of the value of a sovereign], for purposes of remittance they will lose half the value of their salaries." Nicholson's *Money and Monetary Problems.* Page 24.

[3] See pages 45-71.

of the fluctuations in the other.[1] Plainly there is nothing in the nature of things to hinder gold from fluctuating in value whilst the value of silver remains unchanged; nothing to hinder silver from fluctuating in value whilst the value of gold remains unchanged; and, in fine, nothing to hinder both gold and silver from fluctuating in value at the same time, and fluctuating very notably, and in opposite directions.

"This is what we are exposed to in the present Monometallic system. It in no sense results in unity. It results in duality and divergence, pure and simple.

"Now, on the contrary, the aim of the Bimetallists, instead of being—as is sometimes incorrectly supposed—to set up a duality of standards, is to bring about a common standard of value, as far as possible everywhere, in 'gold' countries and 'silver' countries alike. What Bimetallists contend for, in the first place, is that the unity which is one of the first requisites in a monetary standard has not been attained in our present Monometallic system. Furthermore they contend that it can be brought about only by the adoption of the system they advocate, which is, to make the standard of value—if possible everywhere, but, at all events, over the largest possible area amongst the commercial nations of the world—consist, not of one or of the other of the two precious metals, gold or silver, but of a combination of the two, linked together."[2]

[1] See pages 14, 15.
[2] "It seems to me that those who are called Bimetallists are really Monometallists. They try to marry the yellow and the white metal, to combine the two, and thus to create a basis broad enough to carry on the ever increasing commerce of the world, and to found upon it a stable system of prices, and a firm superstructure of credit.

"Those on the other hand, who are called Monometallists are really Bimetallists. They want to divorce silver from gold, and cut the world into two parts with no common measure of value between them'" Speech, *Journal Institute of Bankers*, December 1885, (quoted in *The Silver Question in its Social Aspect*, by Hermann Schmidt: London, 1886. Page 91.)

" But how can two metals be linked together, so as to form, combined, one standard of value ? "

" That is easily shown. Here, for instance, is how they were combined in the system which was in operation in France down to 1873—"

" Down to 1873? Then Bimetallism is not a mere untried theory ? "

" So far from being untried, Bimetallism was at one time in operation in several European countries, and this continued for many years. But there is a special reason for taking the system as it was in operation in France[1] from 1803 to 1873. Bimetallism was established there in 1803 by Napoleon.[1] At that time, the English currency system also was Bimetallist. Bimetallism had been established in England in 1717, on the recommendation of Sir Isaac Newton, then Master of the English Mint. It was not abandoned by England until 1816. But, speaking of France, here is how Bimetallism worked in that country down to 1873. From 1803 to 1873, the French Mint was open for the unrestricted coinage, whether of gold or of silver, either metal being accepted for coinage in the ratio of $15\frac{1}{2}$ to 1,—for instance, $15\frac{1}{2}$ ounces of silver or 1 ounce of gold was coined into an equal sum of money.

---

[1] " The old Bimetallism of Europe was a very rude and unscientific system. There was no unity of action among the nations : each adopted and changed its ratio at will. One nation had 15 to 1 ; another, like England in the last century, had 15.21 to 1, as fixed by Sir Isaac Newton in 1717 ; another had $14\frac{3}{4}$ to 1, and so on . . .

" Besides, there were no open Mints, with unlimited coinage of either metal, which is *the absolute condition of effective Bimetallism* . .

" The second period of Bimetallism was the French system, from 1803 to 1873, which was far more scientific, far more successful in binding the two metals together."—Speech of Mr. Samuel Smith, M.P., in the House of Commons, 18th of April, 1890, see Hansard, 3rd series, vol. 343, page 816.

" In 1865, the same arrangement was adopted by the other countries of the group known as the Latin Union —Belgium, Switzerland, Italy, and Greece.

" Down to 1873, then, anyone, in any part of the world, who had either gold or silver bullion to dispose of, could have taken it to the Mint of any of those countries and there made into coin.

" Here are the three points of the Bimetallic system as it was carried out in those countries. First, any given quantity of gold bullion was always exchangeable at the Mints for its weight in gold coins; and any given quantity of silver bullion was likewise exchangeable for its weight in silver coins. Secondly, the coins given out in return for any weight of standard gold bullion, were of $15\frac{1}{2}$ times the value of those given out in return for the same weight of silver bullion. Thirdly, all those coins, whether of silver or of gold, were ' legal tender,' [1] within the country, for the discharge of all debts, to any amount. [2]

" It can hardly be necessary to point out that when the two metals are thus taken into the standard currency, the fixing of a ratio of value between them,—that is, between the mint value of a given weight of one and the mint

---

[1] See page 22, footnote 1.

[2] The system embodied in the legislation of France from 1803 to 1873 is thus stated by M. Emile de Laveleye.

" The French law of the year 1802 decrees as follows :—

" To every person bringing to this mint 1 kilogramme of gold $\frac{9}{10}$ths fine, this same kilogramme shall be given back to him transformed into 155 gold pieces of 20 francs, the total being equal to 3100 francs.

" To all persons bringing 1 kilogramme of silver $\frac{9}{10}$ths fine, this same kilogramme shall be returned to him coined into 40 five-franc pieces, the total being equal to 200 francs.

" The debtor may tender these gold or silver pieces at his option, and can obtain for them a full receipt for his debt." *The Joint Standard Practically Considered.* By Emile de Laveleye: Manchester and London, 1889, pages 6, 7.

value of the same weight of the other,—is a matter of absolute necessity.

" Except at a fixed ratio of value between them, the two metals could not be kept in circulation in a country as money. That is admitted on all hands. If no check were kept upon the tendencies to divergence between the respective values of gold and silver—the value of each being left to be determined merely by the chances of supply and demand in the markets of the world—commerce would be rendered practically impossible. For it would be open to debtors to discharge their obligations in one or in the other according as one or the other was, for the time, proportionately less in value. That would be utterly subversive of the certainty which is an essential basis of all commercial transactions."

" Whilst the French and other Mints were open for the unlimited coinage of gold and silver, the English Mint was not open in the same way for the coinage of silver to the same extent ? "

" No ; nor for many years before 1873. England had abandoned Bimetallism in 1816, when Lord Liverpool made what every Bimetallist must consider the deplorable mistake of substituting a gold Monometallic system for the Bimetallic system which had been maintained in England ever since its adoption, on the recommendation of Sir Isaac Newton, a hundred years before.

" Since then, silver has been coined in England in limited quantities only. It is not a ' legal tender ' for sums over 40s."

" What, then, are the practical disadvantages of Monometallism ? "

" The first and most obvious objection against a Mono-metallic system of currency is that it leaves the standard of value open in the most unguarded way to the operation of every influence that tends to deprive it of stability. In a Monometallic system, the standard coin, whether it be of gold or of silver, is necessarily exposed to fluctuations in value which may be very considerable and may easily lead to most serious, and even disastrous, results.

" We have already seen that the value of a standard gold or silver coin is simply the value of the metal of which it is composed.[1] Now the value of each of the precious metals, as of any other commodity, is open to wide fluctuations. The value of either of them, like the value of any other commodity, is determined merely by the run of the market, the relation between supply and demand.

" Now, Monometallism, as even the most extreme Monometallists must admit, does nothing to exclude this liability to fluctuation, or even to diminish it. Take, for instance, the English gold Monometallist currency. Gold, and consequently the sovereign,—that is to say, the weight of gold contained in a sovereign,[2]—is liable to fluctuations in value, just as corn is, or cotton, or cloth. Even the most extreme Monometallist will allow that Monometallism does nothing even to check that liability to fluctuation.

" Then there is a second point, the fuller explanation of which may be reserved for a little further on.

" Monometallism, as we have it in Great Britain and Ireland, in Germany, and in so many other countries, tends to raise the value of gold, thereby favouring the interests of all capitalists, the interests of

---

[1] See page 16.   See page 17.

all those who have command of gold—money-lenders
and the like,—favouring all such persons at the expense of the general community, and favouring also the
interests of all creditors, the interests of all who have a
claim to receive a fixed money payment from others,
favouring these at the expense of their unfortunate
debtors."[1]

" But, in England, for instance, where Bimetallism was
abandoned in the early part of this century, no harm
seems to have come of the change—at all events until
recently ? No one seems to have complained ? "

" No, and for a very excellent reason. For, although
the change from Bimetallism to Monometallism was
made in England so far back as 1816, England did
not then feel the effects of the change,—nor indeed
were they felt anywhere,—for many years afterwards.

" They were not, in fact, felt until 1873, when, consequent upon the abandonment by Germany, and other countries, of their former silver standard of currency, and their
adoption of a gold standard, France,—and, with France, the
other countries of the Latin Union,[2]—followed the example
which England had set 47 years before, and closed
their Mints to the free coinage of silver, thus destroying
the link between the two metals and breaking down the
very foundations of the Bimetallic system.

" Until 1873, then, the existence of Bimetallism over the
large area in which it was still maintained, practically
saved the whole commercial world from feeling the effects
of Monometallism. So long as the Mints of so many

[1] See pages 43; 48-50 ; 52, 53 ; 64, 65.   [2] See page 28.

countries were kept open on Bimetallist principles, everything went on almost as before.[1]

"But how could the maintenance of the system in
France and those other countries have affected the relative
values of silver and gold elsewhere? How could it have
affected their relative values, for instance, in England?"

"In this way. Those who had, for example, silver
bullion to dispose of—say, in England—would not part
with 18 or 20 ounces of it for an ounce of gold, when by
sending it to a public mint, in France, for instance, they
could get as valuable an equivalent for 15½ ounces.

"Of course there was some little expense in the trans-
mission from London to Paris. This, and other incidents
of the case, varied slightly from time to time. Hence

[1] "How this uniformity in the relative value of gold and silver was
maintained did not engage the attention of Economists. The fact was
accepted, and it seemed almost an arrangement of nature which the most
violent variations in the relative supplies of the two metals could not disturb.

"But a day came when the true cause of this uniformity was revealed.
The promulgation of a new monetary law at Berlin, and the decision of France
and the Latin Union to suspend the coinage of silver, showed the world that
this uniformity [of ratio between the values of the two metals] had been
dependent on the action of the Bimetallic system of France, backed by the
equilibrium which was maintained by the counteracting influence of silver
Monometallic countries like Germany, as against gold Monometallic
countries such as England.

"With the French law in abeyance, and the general equilibrium
disturbed, the world quickly saw that it was human law, and not [merely] the
natural law of supply and demand, that had linked the two metals so
effectually and so beneficially together." *The Silver Question and the Gold
Question*, by R. Barclay, page 12.

"Capitalists in this country never imagined why this fixity of value
existed—it had been substantially so for nearly two centuries, and it was
supposed to be an ordinance of nature; no one in those days understood that it
was the result of the French Bimetallic system . . .

"We were like a man who never suffered from dyspepsia and hardly
knew he had a stomach, and who first acquired a knowledge of that organ
from a severe fit of indigestion.

"The British public took for granted that gold and silver must somehow
be worth intrinsically as 1 to 15½, in other words that silver naturally fetched
about 5s. an ounce [that is to say, one-fourth of the value of the quantity of the
gold, 123·27447 grains, contained in a sovereign], and it is only the experience
of the last few years that has disabused them of this notion." *The Bimetallic
Question*, by Samuel Smith, M.P. Essay on *Bimetallic Money*, page 15.

the maintenance of the Bimetallic system in France and other countries did not, and could not, keep the values of gold and silver at an absolutely fixed ratio throughout the commercial world.[1] But the fluctuations in their relative value were so slight that the ratio of their values was practically fixed at $15\frac{1}{2}$ to 1.

"During all those years, the oscillations in the relative value of the two metals from the French legal ratio of $15\frac{1}{2}$ to 1 were so slight that, as a rule, they did not pass $15\frac{3}{4}$ to 1, on one side, or $15\frac{1}{4}$ to 1, on the other.

"Thus the fluctuations of value in the monetary standard, not only in the countries of the Latin Union, but elsewhere throughout the whole commercial world, were reduced to a minimum. But in 1873 came the disastrous change. The safety-valve that had been kept open by the action of the French and other mints was then screwed down. So the results of Monometallism at once began to make themselves seriously felt all round, and nowhere more seriously than in Ireland."

"What difference could it make, except, perhaps, in the way of international trade between gold-using and silver-using countries?"

"Even if it affected nothing else, the results might be disastrous. See how it has affected the state of trade between England on the one hand, and India and the other silver-using countries of the East, on the other.

"Take, for example, the great cotton manufacturing industry of Lancashire. Looking into this matter in detail a few days ago, I came across the following figures.

---

[1] "The legal ratio is not an absolute, but a controlling, force, keeping th variation in the market ratio within certain definite limits. *It acts like the governor of a steam engine.*" Speech of Sir W. Houldsworth, M.P., in the House of Commons, 18th of April, 1890. See Hansard, 3rd series, vol. 343, page 838.

From February to August, 1890, the rupee, which, as measured by the sovereign, used to count practically as a two-shilling coin, but had then fallen to 1s. 5d., went up again in value to 1s. 9d. Then, from August, 1890, to February, 1891, it fell from 1s. 9d. again to 1s. 5d. In March last, the exchange value of the rupee dropped so low as 1s. 2⅞d.; and this was a fall of 2½ per cent. within three days !

"As the case, then, was put by one of the speakers at the recent meeting in Manchester, at which Mr. Balfour spoke,[1] the rupture of the link which, until 1873, had kept the proportionate values of gold and silver unchanged, has resulted in such violent and continuous oscillations in the rate of exchange between England and the East—that is to say, between the standard gold coin of England and the standard silver coin of India, the sovereign and the rupee—as to reduce the cotton export trade of Manchester 'almost to a game of chance, . . a gamble in silver, rather than an investment in cottons.'[2]

"And Sir David Barbour, in his Financial Statement for India, for 1891-92, says the same thing, almost in the same words :—

"'Trade between England and India was reduced to mere gambling, the fluctuations in exchange being so great as to more than counterbalance the effect of the other elements which the trader has to take into consideration.

"'It has even been said, with some truth, that at one time *it would have been better for the merchant to dismiss his establishment, and confine himself to speculations in*

---

[1] See pages 3, 4 ; 52, 53.
[2] Speech of Mr. John A. Beith, in the Town Hall, Manchester, on the 27th of October, 1892. (Pamphlet Report of Meeting : London and Manchester, 1892, page 9.)

silver; his expenses would have been less, and his chances of profit quite as good as in his legitimate business."[1]

" But this is not all. The merchant in India who has to pay in rupees cannot afford to go on, year after year, paying more and more rupees for the same quantity of goods.

" For, we must remember, the present state of things is the result of a rise in the value of gold rather than of a fall in the value of silver.[2] Prices, measured by a silver standard of value—as they are measured in India and the other countries of the East—have remained, we may say, unchanged. In India the rupee has undergone practically no loss of purchasing power.

"Whilst the Indian merchant, then—if he continues to buy his goods in England—has to pay 14 or 15 rupees, instead of 10, for every pound's worth, he cannot raise the price to his retail consumers in India.[3] So that, unless the manufacturer in England can reduce his prices, and reduce them so as to cover by the reduction the notable fall that has occurred in the value of the silver rupee as measured by the sovereign—which, of course, he cannot do without a heavy sacrifice of profits, perhaps even without a ruinous loss—the Eastern merchant must give up buying in the English market.

"Now this is what is actually going on from day to day. Trade with the East is rapidly leaving England. Take, for instance, these facts, stated in the speech of Mr. J. A. Beith at the Manchester meeting, from which I have already quoted :—

[1] Quoted in *The Silver Policy of the Government*, by S. Dana Horton : London, 1891.
[2] See pages 45-71.
[3] Mr. Barclay speaks of " the double-faced value, or power of the rupee—its stationary value towards India, and its reduced and fluctuating value towards Europe." *The Silver Question and the Gold Question*, page 118.

" ' Not only has our Eastern trade been retarded, but the practical refusal to take payments in the money of the East except at an enormous discount, has diverted the channels of trade ; and silver-using countries, such as China, have felt themselves compelled to go past Manchester, and to trade with silver-taking countries.[1]

" ' Now the figures on this question are absolutely appalling.

" ' For ten years before this change came [in 1873], Indian mills were in existence, and were working vigorously, and making progress in India ; but during the whole of that ten years they were practically able to export nothing. . . .

" ' In 1874, the total exports of yarn from the Indian mills to China and Japan amounted to only 1,000,000 lbs. It was only in 1875, and when silver had fallen 3*d*. per ounce,[2] that the 1,000,000 lbs. of exports, which it had taken Indian mills nearly ten years to get up to, at once expanded, as if in obedience to the wave of an enchanter's wand, into 5,000,000 lbs.

" ' In 1880 there was a further fall of 5*d*. per ounce,[3] and, consequently, a further advantage to the silver of India and China, as compared with England accepting only gold payments, and so then, the 5 millions of exports from India became 25 millions.

[1] " The Lancashire manufacturer, in order to cope with the fall in exchange, has had to reduce profits to a minimum, and to strive to the utmost in every way to economise production.

" To some extent he has been able to throw the loss on the raw material : but the general result has been that, owing to the difficulty of forcing up prices in India, some kinds of manufacture cannot be sent at all now, and other kinds are subject to most severe competition.

" And when you look beneath the surface of things, that means that, purely owing to monetary changes, *the Indian manufacturer is* . . *protected*." Nicholson, *Money and Monetary Problems*, page 267. See also page 50 of this pamphlet, *footnote* 3.

[2] That is to say, the 'gold price' of silver had fallen. This was the result of a rise, to a proportionate extent, in the value of gold.

[3] See the preceding note.

" ' In 1885, another fall[1] took place, and the 25 millions became 75 millions. In 1889, there was a further fall[2] of 5*d.* in silver, and the 75 millions became 127 millions. In 1891 there was still a further fall,[3] and the 127 millions of exports of yarn from India to China became 165 millions; so that, in 17 years, through the operation of this cause chiefly, 1 million lbs. of yarn exports per annum had risen to 165 million lbs. per annum . . .

" ' This means that India is now sending six times as much as the United Kingdom sends to China and Japan, and twice as much as the United Kingdom sends to India, China, and Japan together.' " [4]

" Then England's loss seems to be India's gain ? "

" Unfortunately the loss is not even compensated for in that way. I do not mean merely that the change in the current of trade brings profit to a small section of English and native capitalists who have invested in Indian mills, rather than to the general population of the country. That indeed is true, but, as regards Indian interests, there is a far more serious aspect of the case.

" There is, in fact, no country in the world, not even Ireland, in which the rupture of the link between gold and silver has proved more disastrous in its results than it has proved in India.

" For, it must always be borne in mind that *India has contracted heavy debts, the interest on which has to be paid in gold.* Whatever profits, then, an increased activity of trade may have brought to India, these are more

[1] See page 36, footnote 2.. [2] See preceding note [3] See preceding note.
[4] Speech of Mr. John A. Beith, in the Town Hall, Manchester, on the 27th October, 1892. (See page 34, *footnote* 2).

than absorbed in providing for the loss which India has to bear on the remittances of cash,—that is to say, from India's having to pay more and more rupees for the gold she has to send to England and elsewhere, in payment of interest.[1]

" In the Report of the Gold and Silver Commission of 1888, the extent of the additional demand thus made upon the Indian Government, that is, in other words, upon the taxpayers of India, is made very plain by the statement that the extra charge resulting from *a fall of even* 1*d. in the exchange*—from the Rupee being worth 1*s.* 5*d.* instead of 1*s.* 6*d.*—amounts to *the enormous sum of* 11,000,000 *of Rupees for the year.* "

" That Commission, then, investigated the question of Bimetallism ? "

" It was, I may say, appointed for that purpose. The Commission was composed of 12 members. They drew up a singularly interesting Report setting forth all the accepted facts of the case, and setting forth also, very fully, the arguments and counter-arguments of Monometallists and Bimetallists on the various facts adduced. That is the first part of the Report. It represents the unanimous view of the Commission. It was signed by the 12 members.

" Then come two supplementary Reports, one signed by the Monometallists members of the Commission, the other by the Bimetallists. But the first portion of the Report, signed unanimously by all 12, might be quoted in support of almost everything I have stated to you, so far.

---

[1] There is, to a certain extent, to be set off against this, the advantage derived by India from the difference of exchange, when Indian exports find a market in gold-using countries. But this covers only a small portion of the general loss.

[2] *Report of the Gold and Silver Commission*, 1888. Part i., n. 106.

" As to the point we are here dealing with, I take the following from that section of the Report which was drawn up by the 6 Monometallist members of the Commission :—

" ' There cannot be two opinions as to the very serious effect which the continued fall in the gold price of silver has had on the finances of the Government of India. Unless expenditure be diminished, every additional fall in the value of the rupee renders additional taxation nesessary if a deficit is to be avoided . . .

" ' We are fully impressed with a sense of the difficulties which surround the Indian Government, and of the serious questions to which any proposed additional tax must give rise.

" ' It is not only the embarrassment which has already been caused to the Government of India that has to be borne in mind, but the impossibility of foreseeing to what extent those embarrassments may be increased, and their difficulty augmented by a further depression.[1] '

" All this was written in October, 1888. Then see how things have been going since then. On the 31st of last March, the following telegram, from its Calcutta correspondent, appeared in *The Times* :—

" ' The continued and unprecedented fall in exchange is causing universal consternation, and threatens to paralyse all trade.

" ' Much indignation is expressed at the apparent apathy of the Home Government.'

" A few days afterwards, *The Times* had the following in a leading article :—

" ' The unprecedented fall in the rupee is causing great

[1] *Report of the Gold and Silver Commission*, 1888. Part ii., nn. 101, 102.

concern to all connected with India. On Friday, our correspondent telegraphed that the feeling in Calcutta was of ' universal consternation.' ' The evil threatens,' he says, ' to paralyze all trades, and much indignation is expressed at the apparent apathy of the Home Government.'

" ' That the position is very serious, and in some respects disastrous, is beyond dispute. . . .

" ' The Government of India finds itself saddled with a currency that is the sport of circumstances over which it has no control.

" ' The effect has been to increase the burden of its public debt, in sterling, by 50 per cent during the past 28 years, quite apart from new borrowings ; to reduce large numbers of its servants to pecuniary distress ; and to affect grain prices in a way which seems, to some observers, to intensify every local failure of the crops, and *to threaten the poorer classes in India with a chronic artificial scarcity of food.*" [1]

" All this makes it very plain what a serious error it would be to suppose that the loss in which the fluctuation in the relative value of the rupee and sovereign has resulted in Lancashire has been made up for by a gain to India.

" Then too, in India, there has been another serious drawback resulting from the present currency arrangements. As a result of the existing state of confusion, it has become impossible for India to obtain the loans that are absolutely necessary for the development of the resources of the country.

" Here is a clear statement on this point :—

" ' The total mileage of railways in India is only

---

[1] *The Times*, April 4th, 1892.

16,996 miles, many of the lines being only for strategic purposes and practically useless for trade ; and the constant cry, for years past, of British merchants, and of those best acquainted with India's requirements, has been for great railway extensions. But the Indian Government, whilst under successive Viceroys recognising these needs, has had to proceed with the work on the smallest possible scale.

" ' The explanation is very simple. It is because the Indian Government has to borrow the cost of construction in gold, and the interest on the debt has to be paid in gold, whilst, on the other hand, the revenue of India is raised in silver.

" ' A fall in exchange, therefore, means that *a larger amount of silver has to be raised to pay the interest on the gold debt.*

" ' To take an extreme case. Suppose a loan of £10.000,000 for an Indian railway had been raised when the rupee was at 2s. That would represent 100 millions of rupees ; and at 4 per cent interest the Indian Government would have to pay the bondholders 4 millions of rupees per annum.

" ' With the rupee at about its present value, however— say 1s. 4d.—the Government would have to raise and pay 6 millions of rupees per annum as interest, *an extra burden of 50 per cent* on the material prosperity of India."

" Last March, *The Times* had a rather interesting article on this aspect of the case :—

" ' Powerful interests in England,' it said, ' demand a more rapid development of railway communication in India . . . On the other hand, the Government wisely

1 *What is the Bimetallic Question ! A Plain Explanation :* London and Manchester, 1892, page 32.

hesitates to impose on the Indian Exchequer the responsibility for gold loans or obligations, which it will have to discharge in a silver currency of vanishing value . . .

"'The truth is that railway development, . . . like the development of every other branch of Indian enterprise, is now *awaiting some settlement as to the future of the rupee*. The currency difficulty *underlies the whole situation*.'[1]

"In the work from which I quoted a few moments ago there is a very pertinent remark about this railway difficulty :—

"' At the present rate of exchange [between the rupee and the sovereign, as compared with the old rate of 2s., or ten rupees to a sovereign], the loss to the Indian Government in remitting [to England] interest on loans, &c., is estimated at about 80,000,000 of rupees per annum. Now those 80 millions of rupees, if they could be saved, would construct, under ordinary conditions, about 1,500 miles of railways per annum, without adding one penny to India's present burden in either capital or interest . . .

"' Every mile of railway constructed there facilitates India's exports, and correspondingly makes a new or a better market for English goods, and, by facilitating food transports, enables us more effectively to provide against the horrors of ever-recurring famines.[2]

"A similar difficulty, it seems, exists in China. It is now not so much ' Celestial ' prejudice, as exchange difficulties, that stop the making of railways in that country. Not long since the Chinese Government endeavoured to raise a loan for railway purposes. But they would only

[1] *The Times*, March 8th, 1892.
[2] *What is the Bimetallic Question? A Plain Explanation*. London and Manchester, page 33.

raise it in silver, and have it payable both as to capital and interest in silver. European financiers, under the present monetary arrangements of the commercial world, would not entertain the transaction.

" India, of course, is loudly clamouring for the removal of the difficulty in the only way in which it can really be removed, that is, by a revival of the former Bimetallic currency arrangements which were departed from in 1873.

" But then, account has to be taken of the dogged resistance that indubitably will be offered to any such measure of reform, by the capitalists, the money-owners and the money-lenders of the world. It is their interest to prop up the present system of currency.[1] That system, no doubt, in countless ways, grinds the faces of the poor. But what matter? It is all to the profit of the owners and holders of gold.[2] So the owners and holders of gold will hold on by it to the death.

" It is little wonder, then, that in view of the tremendous opposition sure to be offered by all such persons, the re-establishment of Bimetallism should have come to be looked upon as an almost Utopian idea.

" But then, what other remedy for the undeniable and unquestionable evil of the present state of affairs is to be looked for?

---

[1] See pages 48-50 ; 52, 53.

[2] This view of the case was dealt with, in language of strong indignation, by Mr. Samuel Smith, M.P., in his speech on the debate on Bimetallism in the House of Commons in the session of 1890:—

" There is much reason to suspect that there was a kind of conspiracy among the financial class in Europe and America to get altogether rid of silver as full-valued money, in order to increase the value of gold.

" Their aim was to bring about a universal gold standard. *They calculated on the ignorance of the masses about all monetary questions*, and very nearly succeeded, for a time, in what I could only call a nefarious plot.

" I believe it is largely owing to the efforts of the Bimetallic party that the tendency to demonetise silver has been checked, and a gigantic fraud against civilisation has not been fully consummated." See Hansard, 3rd series, vol. 343, pages 822, 3.

" Apart from the re-establishment of Bimetallism, the only other practical[1] policy that has been proposed—and it has been proposed only as a remedy for the special evils arising out of the difficulty about exchange between gold-using and silver-using countries, such as England and India—is the adoption of a gold standard for India.

" From a belief very generally entertained, that the British Government is too far committed to Monometallism to leave any immediate likelihood of its immediately retracing its steps, the adoption of a gold standard for India has been suggested.

" But the adoption of a gold standard for India is a policy which even *The Times*—strongly Monometallist as its present financial tendency is—shrinks from advocating. ' It is an alternative,' says *The Times,* ' fraught with financial difficulties, and with derangements to the existing basis of Indian commerce and manufactures, which any Government may well shrink from encountering.' "[2]

" But would it not seem a useful thing to bring about a unity of monetary standard at all events between India and England, and possibly between all ' gold-using ' and all ' silver-using ' countries ? "

" Yes ; but how can it be done except through the restoration of Bimetallism ? As for the adoption of a gold standard for India, the result would be disaster all round. This reference to the prospect of the adoption by India of a gold Monometallist currency, brings us to the consideration of another grave result of our present Monometallist system,—one of the very gravest results of it,—a result far more widely extended, and far more calamitous in its influence, than any of those which we have, so far, been considering.

[1] See pages 92-96.   [2] *The Times,* March 8th, 1892.

" It is to be borne in mind, then, that money
has to serve, not merely as a medium of exchange
in the purchase of commodities, but also as a measure
and record of the extent of obligations in the case of
all deferred payments, or of payments extending over
long periods—as, for instance, the yearly payments of
rent or of the interest on a mortgage.

" Now it can hardly need to be pointed out that, so long
as contracts into which time enters as an element are
expressed in terms of money, it is of the utmost importance
that the monetary standard should, as far as possible, be
stable in value. Absolute stability of value is, as we
have seen, unattainable.[1] But, in its absence, comparative
stability is to be looked for, as one of the first requisites in
a monetary standard.

" As Mr. Barclay puts it, 'the value of money might
vary without much inconvenience if all transactions were
immediate exchanges in which money simply prevented
a resort to barter. But, as we know, the whole structure of
trade is based on credit and time contracts; and, in view of
this, the medium of exchange, which is also a standard of
value, *cannot vary without inflicting serious injury either
upon debtor or creditor.*'[2] Stability of value, then, in so far
as it is attainable, is an all-important element of money.

" Now it is in this point especially that our present
Monometallist system of currency is open to most serious
objection.

" Gold, as the result of a variety of causes, is steadily
and seriously increasing in value. And not merely does
Monometallism provide no check upon this increase, but

---

[1] See page 15.
[2] *The Silver Question and the Gold Question*, by R. Barclay, page 54.

the increase itself is, in great part, the result of the changes that have been made in so many countries, in the direction of Monometallism, within the last twenty years.

"The chief source of the notable rise that has taken place in the value of gold is the heavy additional demand which, from various causes, has fallen upon gold during these later years. One of those disturbing causes, for instance, was the closing of the French and other European Mints in 1873 against the unrestricted coinage of silver.[1] Another was the adoption, about the same time, of a gold standard of currency in Germany, and in several other countries which, until then, had retained a silver standard.[2] All this led to an enormous extra demand upon gold, and consequently to a very notable increase in the value of gold.[3]

"The necessary result of this increase in value is that our present monetary standard of value has become an altogether misleading standard. As gold began steadily to go up in value, every existing obligation to pay a fixed amount of pounds, shillings, and pence,[4] became more and more burdensome than before.

"This, then, told heavily against all debtors, and gave an undue advantage to all creditors.[5]

"As I have elsewhere made special reference to the disastrous results of the change in the case of our Irish farmers, I ought not to omit to state that, from another

---

[1] See page 31.   [2] *Ibid.*   [3] See pages 16, 17.   [4] See pages 14-19.
[5] "What every honest man should aim at is stability in the standard of value, so that debtors shall not be obliged to pay more than they stipulated, nor creditors compelled to accept less.

"Now what is actually happening in England, and in all other countries having a gold standard is this—the debtor class is paying the creditor class more than it intended to do when the debts were contracted." *The Bimetallic Question.* By Samuel Smith, M.P. : London, 1887. Essay on *Gold and Silver and the Depression of Trade*, page 90.

side, the landlords' interests have been affected at least as seriously as those of the tenants. No class in the community indeed has suffered more disastrously from the change than the owners of land charged with mortgages, as, unfortunately, the greater part of the land of Ireland is charged to an oppressively burdensome extent.

" But, within certain limits, this source of difficulty exists, not only in Ireland, but in England also.

" ' The landlords,' says Mr. Samuel Smith, ' who borrowed 400 millions on their property, agreeing to pay, let us say, 16 millions a-year interest at 4 per cent, supposing that it represented one-fourth of their rents, now find, owing to the fall of prices, that it represents one-third, or even in some cases one-half, of their rents.[1]

" Then, manufacturers and traders, too, have suffered, and suffered heavily. ' The factory-owner,' continues Mr. Smith, ' the mine-owner, the ship-owner, who thought it safe twenty years ago to borrow half the value of his plant in order to find capital for his business, now finds that the mortgagee is the virtual owner. Nearly all the profits go to pay the mortgagee's claim, and in many cases he has foreclosed and sold up the unhappy borrower, ruined through no fault of his own, but solely through the extraordinary sinking of prices. . .

" ' As a matter of fact, I believe that if all the fixed capital engaged in trade in England could be valued to-day at its real selling price, it would be found that it would do little more than pay the mortgages and debts upon it.' [2]

[1] *The Bimetallic Question*, by Samuel Smith, M.P. : London, 1887. Essay on *Gold and Silver and the Depression of Trade*, page 90.
[2] *Ibid.*, pages 90, 91.

"The following passage from the same writer is also well worth quoting. It brings out, very plainly, another of the ways in which Monometallism has worked mischief, by the depressing influence which the increase in the value of gold has exercised upon trade :—

"'Trade is very greatly and injuriously affected by a sudden alteration in the standard of value, especially when the alteration is, as now, towards increased value.

"'It arises in this way. Trade is largely carried on by borrowed capital, or, in other words, by the use of credit in some shape or other ; the vast banking deposits are mostly lent to traders ; a very great deal of the invested capital of this country is lent upon mortgage of trading property, such as ships, factories, warehouses, &c.

"'A prudent trader usually considers it safe to trade considerably beyond his floating capital, and to borrow, say, 50 per cent on the security of his plant or fixed capital. Now the constant decline of prices, the last few years, has virtually swept away his own portion of the capital, and only left him enough to pay the loans and mortgages.

"'For instance, a ship or a factory built at a cost of £20,000, of which £10,000 was borrowed, is now worth only £12,000, or 40 per cent less ; and so the mortgage represents five-sixths of the value instead of one-half, the trader's interest having sunk to £2,000, in place of £10,000. Probably, if trade is unprofitable, he fails to pay the interest, and the mortgage is foreclosed ; the property is forced off at just sufficient to cover the loan, and he is ruined.

"'I have no doubt that this process exactly describes the condition of vast numbers of the traders of this country and of other countries having a gold standard.

"'A great portion of the commercial capital of the country has passed into the hands of the mortgagees and bondholders, who have neither toiled nor spun. The discouragement this state of things produces is intense. After it has gone on for several years, a kind of hopelessness oppresses the commercial community, all enterprise comes to a standstill, many works are closed, labour is thrown out of employment, and great distress is felt both among labourers and the humbler middle class. Indeed, it strikes higher than this; for multitudes of people who once were prosperous traders have now become depending on charity. I know many such myself.'[1]

"Then the case of the National Debts and various local and other debts[2] of the various nations of the world furnish

---

[1] *The Bimetallic Question*, by Samuel Smith, M.P. Answers to Questions issued by the Royal Commission on the Depression of Trade and Industry, pages 210-12.

[2] "Is the House aware of the heavy burden under which the trade of this country is carried on? I do not think many people are aware of it, but I have taken pains for years past to ascertain what the charges upon our trade and commerce really are, and I put it that the trade of the country is carried on under a vast burden of fixed charges, payable in gold, amounting certainly to not less than £150,000,000 a-year, and probably as much as £200,000,000 a-year.

"These include national and local debts, mortgages, ground rents, mining royalties, railway debentures and preference shares, long leases, annuities, pensions, &c.

"The purchasing power of gold is about 40 per cent greater than it was in 1873, that is to say, 40 per cent more of the products of human industry have to be sold to raise the needful to meet these charges.

"This is a tax levied by the drones on the working bees of society, and surely it cannot for the well-being of society to add to the incomes of the idle non-producing class at the cost of the toiling masses.

"I hold that one-half of this extra burden is the result of the demonetisation of silver: had these metals continued to be tied together by the Bimetallic Law of 15½ to 1, the fall of prices would have been equally diffused over both gold and silver using countries . . . The creditor class, the wealthy bondholders, money-lenders, mortgagees, &c., would have lost one-half of their unearned increment, which would have remained in the pockets of the wealthy industrial class, who constitute 90 per cent of the nation.

"This one-half cannot be put at less than £30,000,000 a-year." (Speech of Mr. Samuel Smith, M.P., in the House of Commons, April 18th, 1860. See Hansard, 3rd series, vol. 343, pages 821, 2.)

another instance of the evil resulting to the general community from a rise in the value of gold.[1]

"As to the National Debt of England, Mr. S. Dana Horton in his valuable work, 'The Silver Pound,' calculates, on the basis of figures collected by eminent statisticians, that 'the National Debt, regarded as a principal sum, has increased its weight upon the shoulders of the British taxpayer between 1875 and 1885 *by nearly* 200 *millions sterling*, an amount *nearly equalling the Franco-German war fine.'*[2]

"And we have to remember that, as regards especially National Debts, the national creditors are represented mainly by the capitalist and money-owning classes,[3] whilst the principal representatives of the national debtors are those who labour in the fields, the factories, or the mines.[4]

[1] " It is a foolish reply to this that the aggregate wealth of the nation is not changed, because it is only a transfer from one class to another ; one might as well say that the craft of the pickpocket or cardsharper is innocuous, because it only transfers wealth from one pocket to another.
" The prosperity of the nation depends upon the just distribution of wealth, and the security of industry ; nothing affects it more vitally than unjust alienation."—*The Bimetallic Question*, by Samuel Smith, M.P. *Answers to Questions on Currency and Prices*, page 113.

[2] *The Silver Pound.* By S. Dana Horton. London. 1887, page 11.

[3] " The most plausible objection brought against us, and the one which most easily excites vulgar prejudice, is, that we favour Protection.
" I must ask to say a word or two about this. I utterly disclaim for myself, the slightest desire to bring about Protection : all I wish is a just monetary standard, which will be best attained by using the two metals jointly, instead of one of them singly . . .
" If the question of Protection is to be introduced into the discussion, then it will be found to tell more forcibly against our opponents. What do they seek for but the protection of gold as against silver ? They wish, as far as lies in their power, to ' boycot ' silver, and throw the world upon gold alone, even though such a course should double the value of gold . . .
" In trying to boycot silver, *they are giving Protection to the wealthy capitalist class just as clearly as the old Corn Laws did to the landowners of this country.* The only difference is that the amounts involved are much larger, and the protected class much richer, and the confiscation of the fruits of the toilers much more sweeping, than under the old system of the Corn Laws.
" When the masses of this country awake, as those of America have awaked, to the magnitude of this question, they will brush away this idle talk that we are trying to restore Protection." (Speech of Mr. Samuel Smith, M.P., in the House of Commons, April 18th, 1892: see Hansard, 3rd series, Vol. 343. pages 833, 4.)

[4] See *The Standard of Value.* By W. L. Jordan, London, 1882, page 56.

" In this way, then, the Irish farmers too have suffered ?

" Yes ; that is, those farmers who have rents fixed under leases, or rents judicially fixed for 15 years, or those who are under any such obligation of making fixed payments from year to year. The case of the tenant-purchasers under any of the Land Purchase Acts is one of special hardship. In their case, the obligation of the annual payments extends over, not merely 15, but 49 years.[1]

" Here is where the difficulty comes in. In all such cases, the farmer is under the obligation of paying, year after year, an amount specified in pounds, shillings, and pence. But then this rent, or other annual payment which he has to make, though it is thus specified in amount, is really increasing, that is to say, *becoming more burdensome from year to year.*[2]

" To bring the matter to a point, it comes to this, that, year after year, more corn, more hay, more cattle, have to be sold by the farmer to enable him to get the gold which is required to meet that annual payment.

" But, of course, if he has not more corn, more hay, or more cattle to sell, he cannot, out of what he has to sell, get enough to enable him to make that payment.

" And, plainly, the longer the term for which his ' fixed ' annual payment has to be made, the more disastrous must the results be to him."

" Then the foreign competition, of which we hear so much, is not the sole cause of the ruinous fall in agricultural prices ? "

" No. It is, no doubt, one element in the case. But, as everything goes to show, the main cause of the ruinous fall in agricultural, as in other prices, is the

[1] See pages 2, 3 : 8 : 10.   [2] See pages 9-12 : 45, 46.

continuous increase in the value of gold—the 'appreciation' of gold, as that increase in value is called in the jargon of the political economists.

" Now this brings us to the point in Mr. Balfour's Manchester speech, to which I would specially direct attention.

" 'Money,' said Mr. Balfour. " has to serve, not merely as a medium of exchange, but also as 'a fair and permanent record of obligations extending over long periods of time.' In this, which he rightly called a 'great and fundamental requirement,' our existing currency, as he declared with emphasis, 'totally and lamentably fails.'

"To make good this statement, Mr. Balfour pointed out that the gold monetary standard of Great Britain and Ireland has, in some 15 or 16 years, gone up in value no less than 30 or 35 per cent ; and he went on to say that, of its further progressive appreciation, or rise in value, ' *no man living can prophecy the limits.*' Again, he spoke of the increase in value of our present Monometallist gold standard of value, as progressing 'steadily, continuously, indefinitely.'

"As to the result of all this upon the community generally, Mr. Balfour expressed himself as follows :—

" ' If you will show me a system which gives . . . absolute permanence, I will take it in preference to any other. But *of all conceivable systems of currency*, that system is *assuredly the worst*, which gives you a standard steadily, continuously, indefinitely appreciating, and which by that very fact *throws a burden upon every man of enterprise*, upon every man who desires to promote the agricultural

---

¹ Speech by the Right Hon. A. J. Balfour, in the Town Hall, Manchester, 27th October, 1892 (Pamphlet Report of Meeting : London and Manchester, 1892, pages 30, 31).

or the industrial resources of the country, and *benefits no human being whatever but the owner of fixed debts in gold.'*

" But this was nothing new.   Mr. Balfour's views were on record, years before.   There is a highly important statement from him, and from five other members of the Royal Commission, the Gold and Silver Commission,[1] of 1887.

" In the special Report drawn up by the 6 Bimetallist members of that Commission—including Mr. Balfour and Mr. Chaplin, two members of the late Cabinet—a distinct reference is made to the question of rents.   Speaking of ' *leases for long terms of years,* annuities, pensions, and other similar charges,' they say that ' with every rise in the value of gold, *the weight of this burden upon the industry of the country* increases.'

" What a prospect this is for Irish tenants with ' judicial ' rents fixed for 15 years, or for tenant-purchasers with their annual payments to the Government fixed for the next 49 years ! [2]

" As I am speaking of Mr. Balfour, it may be interesting to note that his Irish Land Purchase Act contains a very efficient, if somewhat elaborate, provision for the protection of the State against loss, in the event, by no means unlikely, of the purchasing tenant breaking down in his payments before the 49 years are out.

" In the scheme embodied in Mr. Balfour's Purchase Act, the purchasing tenant has to begin by paying at an extra rate for a number of years, so as to build up a substantial guarantee fund for the State.

" No wonder, indeed, that Mr. Balfour, Bimetallist as he is, should have clearly seen the necessity for some

---

[1] See page 38.   [2] See pages 2, 3 ; 8 ; 10.

such provision. By most people it seems to have been looked upon as a mere superfluity of complication.

"Mr. Balfour, however, was in a position to see, what, of course, the general public were wholly unaware of, that a payment which a purchasing tenant may now be in a position to make—or which he may be in a position to make for the next few years—may be altogether beyond his reach in probably 10 or 12 years to come. Putting on the screw for the first few years, then, is good policy. If it is not good for the tenant, it is good for the State. Whatever may befal the unfortunate tenant-purchaser, the State at all events is somewhat safeguarded. It has a better chance of getting back the money it has advanced.

"As for the tenant-purchaser, he probably thinks that, after the extra pressure of the first few years, he may look forward to easy times for the rest of his life. He little knows what is before him. If things go on as they are, it will be harder for him, 10 or 12 years hence, to pay £40 a-year, than it would be for him to pay £50 a-year now. But of all this, he knows nothing. How could he? His only idea is that a pound is always a pound, a sovereign always a sovereign. So, in the belief that the yearly payment, when it is reduced to £40, will be well within his reach, he puts his head into the halter.

"But we must be fair. No one can say that Mr. Balfour used his general knowledge of the financial situation to entrap the tenants unawares. He did nothing of the kind. If they did not know what was before them, they cannot blame Mr. Balfour for it. He never concealed his views. He did not fail to give them plain warning of the consequences of entering into prolonged obligations for the payment of fixed amounts.

"What he said quite recently at the meeting in Manchester is, perhaps, in one sense, somewhat more explicit:

but it is not in any way different in sense or substance from what he had said, years before, in the most formal and public way, in the Report of the Gold and Silver Commission of 1888.[1]

"I have thought it important to call attention to the published statements of Mr. Balfour's views on this matter. His position as a prominent politician, especially in view of his recent official connection with Ireland, makes them of special interest. But they are in no way different from those expressed by many others who have written or spoken on the subject.

"Mr. Samuel Smith, for instance, in an essay on 'The Sufferings caused by the Appreciation of the Gold Standard,' calls special attention to the increasing burden thrown upon agricultural tenants by the maintenance of the present Monometallic system. He speaks more especially of the Irish tenants, in view of the fact that so many of them are in the embarrassing position of having rents judicially fixed for 15 years.[2]

"This aspect of the case is brought out forcibly also by the Belgian economist, Emile de Laveleye :—

"'This consideration,' he says, ' especially affects Ireland . . .

"'If you can let tenants hold their land for nothing, it would be all right; but if they have to pay a fair rental either to landlords or to the Government, or to purchase at a fair price, they must then sell produce so as to procure the amount requisite for purchase or for a fair rent.

"'If the price of this produce is very low, and is falling

---

[1] See page 38.
[2] See *The Bimetallic Question*. By Samuel Smith, M.P.: London 1887, pages 134-6.

still lower, then the tenants will be incapable of raising the required sum, and it will be necessary to evict them . . . or to cancel their debts.

"'The supply of gold being wholly insufficient, a fall in prices must ensue ; hence *the ruin of Irish cultivators, in spite of Home Rule.*'

"So far, then, for the chief source of the evils of our present Monometallist system, and the wide field throughout which the calamitous influence makes itself felt. It remains only to point out in what way Bimetallism provides a safeguard against these manifold evils—"

"But, first, as to the fundamental fact, the rise in the value of gold. What do the Monometallists say as to the existence of an extra demand upon gold, and a consequent rise in its value ?"

"That, no doubt, is a point of much importance, especially in view of the disastrous bearing of the present currency system upon Irish farmers.

"For a long time, the truth of the proposition so emphatically proclaimed by the Bimetallists—that the pressure upon the existing supply of gold was increasing, and that gold, consequently, was increasing in value— was disputed by Monometallists.

If, indeed, the Monometallists, at the outset, were committed to anything, they were committed to this, that there was no serious difficulty about gold—that is, in other words, that there was no embarrassing extra demand upon gold in relation to the existing supply of it

---

¹ *The Joint Standard Practically Considered.* Address by Emile de Laveleye, delivered at an International Monetary Congress, Paris, October, 13th, 1889 : Manchester and London, 1889.

—and that, consequently, the present general fall in prices should be ascribed, not to a change in the value of the metal which forms our only standard of value, but to an indefinite number of other causes, happening, somehow, all of them, to work together in the same direction.[1] Silver, they said, was going down in value. Other commodities, generally, were going down in value. But gold, they maintained, was practically steady.

" Now, however, there are not many intelligent Mono-metallists who would care to identify themselves with the maintenance of such statements.

" No Bimetallist, indeed, has written more conclusively in refutation of the old Monometallist view upon this funda-mental point than Mr. Giffen, the well-known Chief of the Statistical Department of the Board of Trade, probably the most determined and uncompromising champion of Monometallism in England.[2]

" In a statistical paper of exceptional interest," read by Mr. Giffen before the Royal Statistical Society in London, in 1888, he not merely accepted, but proclaimed with marked emphasis, the proposition that gold had notably gone up in purchasing power ; that the increase was continuing, and was likely to continue ; and that this increase in the purchasing power of gold gives the true ex-planation of the fall in the price of commodities generally.

" Mr. Giffen, indeed, in that paper, was not satisfied with dealing with the state of things as they were then found to exist. He claimed, and apparently not

See pages 78, 79.
[2] See pages 84-86.
[3] *Recent Changes in Prices and Incomes Compared.* By Robert Giffen, London, 1888.

without justice, that a prediction of his in this matter had come true.

" In a former paper, read in 1879, he had, he said, pointed out the likelihood that a rise in the purchasing power of gold would soon become evident, and he had said that if this were to occur, there were sufficient facts in the diminished supply of gold, and in the increased demands upon gold, to account for the increase in its purchasing power.'

" Then, in his paper of 1888, he went on to say :— 'If the test of prophecy be the event, there was never surely a better forecast. The fall of prices in such a general way as to amount to what is known as *a rise in the purchasing power of gold*, is generally—*I might almost say, universally*—admitted. . . .

" 'Measured by any commodity, or group of commodities, usually taken as the measure for such a purpose, *gold is undoubtedly possessed of more purchasing power than was the case* 15 *or* 20 *years ago*, and this high purchasing power has been continued over a long enough period to allow for all minor oscillations.' [2]

" In the same paper, Mr. Giffen deals very fully with the evidence of all this, furnished by the statistics of the fall in prices of the leading commodities. [3] The comparison is worked out by a well-known method, that of 'Indexnumbers.'

" An 'Index-number' is a device to enable an average to be struck of the prices of a great number of articles.

" There are several sets of such numbers, worked out by statisticians, and brought up to date each year. The *Economist* newspaper gives a set based upon the whole-

[1] *Recent Changes in Prices and Incomes Compared.* By Robert Giffen : London, 1888, pages 7 and 8.
[2] *Ibid.*, page 8.   [3] See page 20, *footnote.*

sale prices of 22 of the principal articles in the London
Market. An eminent statistician, Mr. A. Sauerbeck, has
worked out a set upon a far broader basis, 45 articles
being included.

"Here is a Table showing the almost continuous
fall in the wholesale prices of commodities, as represented by the 45 principal commodities comprised in
Mr. Sauerbeck's computation. I give the Index-numbers
of Mr. Sauerbeck's Table, from 1874 to 1892 :—

Years	Mr. Sauerbeck's Index-numbers for 45 principal Commodities
1874	102
1875	96
1876	95
1877	94
1878	87
1879	83
1880	88
1881	85
1882	84
1883	82
1884	76
1885	72
1886	69
1887	68
1888	70
1889	72
1890	72
1891	72
1892	68

"In the Report of the Gold and Silver Commission
of 1888,[1] Mr. Sauerbeck's Index-numbers are given in an

[1] See page 38.

ingenious arrangement, the average of the numbers for a continuous period of 10 years being given from year to year. The following is a section of the Table, commencing with the period of 10 years which has for its middle point the beginning of the year 1874 :—

For the period 1869-78, average of the ten yearly numbers, 99

,,	1870-79	,,	,,	,,	97
,,	1871-80	,,	..	,,	96
..	1872-81	,,	,,	,,	95
,,	1873-82	..	,.		93
..	1874-83		..	,.	90
	1875-84	..	..	..	87
..	1876-85	..	,.		85
	1877-86		.,	..	82
,,	1878-87		,.	.,	79

"This may be a convenient place to mention that Mr. Sauerbeck has worked out also the yearly Index-numbers of the price of silver. These numbers are instructive under two aspects. First, they show the remarkable steadiness in the gold price[1] of silver so long as the Bimetallic system of the Latin union was in operation,[2] as contrasted with the notable fall that has since taken place. Secondly, they bring into marked prominence the wonderful similarity between the fall in the gold price of commodities in general,[3] and the fall in the gold price of silver.

"To bring out this second point, it is enough to tabulate the respective Index-numbers for the years from 1874 to 1892. But to bring out the first point, it is necessary to take two periods, one preceding, the other following, the year of the disastrous change.

"The following Table, then, sets forth, by means of Mr. Sauerbeck's Index-numbers, the striking contrast

---

[1] See pages 19-21. [2] See pages 27, 28. [3] See page 20, *footnote*.

between the relative value of gold and silver in the
years preceding, and in the years following, 1873.

Years from 1873 back to 1854.	Yearly Index-numbers of Silver	Yearly Index-numbers of Silver	Years from 1873 on to 1892.
1873	97.4	97.4	1873
1872	99.2	95.8	1874
1871	99.7	93.3	1875
1870	99.6	86.7	1876
1869	99.6	90.2	1877
1868	99.6	86.4	1878
1867	99.7	84.2	1879
1866	100.5	85.9	1880
1865	100.3	85.0	1881
1864	100.9	84.9	1882
1863	101.1	83.1	1883
1862	100.9	83.3	1884
1861	99.9	79.9	1885
1860	101.4	74.6	1886
1859	102.0	73.3	1887
1858	101.0	70.4	1888
1857	101.5	70.2	1889
1856	101.0	78.4	1890
1855	100.7	74.1	1891
1854	101.1	65.4	1892

" Taking, then, the two equal periods of 19 years, one
preceding 1873, the other subsequent to that year, we find
that in the former period, during which the Bimetallic
system of the Latin Union was in operation,[1] the extreme
range of the gold price[2] of silver lay between 102.0 and
99.2 ; whilst, throughout the period following the abandonment of that system in 1873, there has been a persistent
fall, the Index-numbers ranging down through the nineties,

See pages 27, 28.   [2] See pages 19-21.

the eighties, and the seventies, and reaching at length to the low figure of 65.4.

"The contrast between the practical stability of the gold price of silver during the period preceding 1873, and its utter instability since then, may be exhibited in perhaps a still more striking form by indicating, for each year, *the difference* by which the Index-number of the price of silver for the year *exceeded, or fell short of*, 100.

" This is shown in the following Table :—

19 Years preceding 1873.		19 Years following 1873.	
Years	Difference between the yearly Index-number of Silver and 100	Difference between the yearly Index-number of Silver and 100	Years
1872	— 0.8	— 4.2	1874
1871	— 0.3	— 6.7	1875
1870	— 0.4	— 13.3	1876
1869	— 0.4	— 9.8	1877
1868	— 0.4	— 13.6	1878
1867	— 0.3	— 15.8	1879
1866	+ 0.5	— 14.1	1880
1865	+ 0.3	— 15.0	1881
1864	+ 0.9	— 15.1	1882
1863	+ 1.1	— 16.9	1883
1862	+ 0.9	— 16.7	1884
1861	— 0.1	— 21.1	1885
1860	+ 1.4	— 25.4	1886
1859	+ 2.0	— 26.7	1887
1858	+ 1.0	— 29.6	1888
1857	+ 1.5	— 29.8	1889
1856	+ 1.0	— 21.6	1890
1855	+ 0.7	— 25.9	1891
1854	+ 1.1	— 34.6	1892

" Then the wonderful similarity—allowance being made for the inevitable slight divergence in detail—between the fall in the gold price[1] of silver and the fall in the gold price of commodities in general,[2] is shown in the following Table.

"This Table gives, in parallel columns, for the years 1874--92, (1) the Index-numbers for the 45 commodities comprised in Mr. Sauerbeck's computation, and (2) the Index-numbers of silver for the same years:—

Years	Mr. Sauerbeck's Index-numbers.	
	Index-number of 45 Principal Commodities	Index-number of Silver
1874	102	95.8
1875	96	93.3
1876	95	86.7
1877	94	90.2
1878	87	86.4
1879	83	84.2
1880	88	85.9
1881	85	85.0
1882	84	84.9
1883	82	83.1
1884	76	83.3
1885	72	79.9
1886	69	74.6
1887	68	73.3
1888	70	70.4
1889	72	70.2
1890	72	78.4
1891	72	74.1
1892	68	65.4

"It is sufficient to note that, in one case, the Index-numbers show a fall from 102 to 68, and, in the other, a fall from 95 to 65. What more striking evidence could be looked for, that the fall, all round, is the result, not of causes

[1] See pages 19-21.   [2] See page 20, *footnote.*

affecting merely the prices of commodities on the one hand, nor of causes affecting merely the price of silver on the other, but of the one cause that influences both alike ; that is to say, a progressive increase of value in the standard, gold, in reference to which the prices, whether of commodities or of silver, are stated ?

" Returning to Mr. Giffen's paper,[1] I should not omit to remark that he puts very plainly the inevitable effects of the fall in prices—or, in other words, the inevitable effects of the rise in the purchasing power of gold—which is thus disclosed.

" ' It is obvious,' he says, ' beyond all question, that these effects may be important. . . *The weight of all permanent burdens is increased* as compared with what would have been the case if there had been no appreciation.

" ' People in paying annuities, or old debts, have to give sovereigns—which each represent a greater quantity of commodities, a greater quantity of the results of human energy, than it would have represented if there had been no appreciation. . .

" ' *The debtors pay more* than they would otherwise pay, and *the creditors receive more.* . . Appreciation'— that is, in other words, an increase in the value, or purchasing power, of the standard coin —' is a most serious matter to those who have debts to pay.'[2]

" Mr. Giffen then went on to speculate as to the future. ' I am,' he said, ' bound to say that *all the evidence seems to me to point to a continuance of the appreciation.* . . It is impossible to suppose that the movement [for the adoption of a gold standard of currency] will not extend to other

[1] See pages 57, 58.
[2] *Recent Changes in Prices and Incomes Compared.* By Robert Giffen. London, 1888, page 47.

countries. . . All these facts point to *a continued pressure on gold.* . . The better probability seems to be that *the increase of the purchasing power of gold will continue from the present time.'* [1]

" Here, in fact, we have, in another form, the statement made by Mr. Balfour in his recent speech in Manchester. Mr. Balfour spoke of our present gold standard of value as having gone up in value " no less than 30 or 35 per cent in some 15 or 16 years; " and again he says of it that it still is " steadily, continuously, and indefinitely " increasing in value, so that " no man living" can " prophecy the limits ' to which the increase may not extend.[2]

" It is true that, about a year after the publication of the important paper from which I have been quoting, Mr. Giffen—taken aback, the Bimetallists say, by discovering the extent to which his statistical paper had strengthened their hands in the currency controversy—wrote a paper in the *Nineteenth Century* in a diametrically opposite sense.[3] But no one seems to have taken that paper seriously. Mr. Giffen, so far from giving any reasons for his astounding change of front, did not even write as if he was aware that he was making any change of front at all. He simply struck out in a diametrically opposite direction, ignoring all that he had said in his statistical paper, all the facts and figures that he had marshalled in that paper with such logical force.

[1] *Recent Changes in Prices and Incomes Compared.* By Robert Giffen ; London, 1888, page 47.
" I should like to add," said Mr. Samuel Smith, in his speech in the debate on Bimetallism in the House of Commons in 1890, " that no one has written more ably on the subject of the appreciation of our gold standard, and the injury that it does to the debtor class, than Mr. Giffen, who has . . shown such unaccountable hostility to our movement." Hansard, third series, vol, 343, page 824.
[2] Speech of the Right Hon. A. J. Balfour, in the Town Hall, Manchester, 27th October, 1892. (Pamphlet Report of the Meeting: London and Manchester, 1892, page 30.)
[3] "A Problem in Money," by Robert Giffen—(*The Nineteenth Century*, November, 1889. pp. 863-81.)

"Mr. Giffen's paper in the *Nineteenth Century*, was not a statistical paper in any sense. It was simply a disquisition on the currency question on grounds of abstract political economy. Now Mr. Giffen is a statistician, and not a political economist. In his paper, then, in the *Nineteenth Century*, he propounds, as might have been expected, some sensationally novel views. He does not even seem to have been aware of their novelty.

"Professor Nicholson showed up all this, in triumphant fashion, in the next number of the *Nineteenth Century*,[1] and, so far as I know, Mr. Giffen has never even attempted to reply. His expedition into the realms of political economy has ended, in fact, in a lamentable collapse.

"But, whatever fate may befal Mr. Giffen's philosophical ventures, his statistical paper of 1888, on the appreciation or increase in purchasing power, of gold, and the disastrous effect of this increase upon all who have debts to pay,[2] holds its ground. I understand that he has omitted that paper from a volume of his essays collected for republication. It would be much more to the point if he were to endeavour to neutralize the effect of it—in the supposition that he is in a position to do so—by pointing out any error he had discovered in it, either in his statement of the statistics of the case, or in his inferences from them.

"So long as that paper stands unrefuted by Mr. Giffen himself, he must submit to be claimed as a prominent witness to the facts upon which Bimetallism is based.

"Mr. Giffen, in his statistical paper of 1888, refers exultingly, as I have mentioned,[3] to a previous paper written by him nine years before. An interesting point connected with that earlier paper of his is the important

---

[1] "Mr. Giffen's Attack on Bimetallists" by Professor Nicholson (*The Nineteenth Century*, December, 1889, pp. 1014-23).
[2] See pages 57-65.   [3] See pages 57-58.

reference made to it by Mr. Goschen in a convincing address, delivered before the Institute of Bankers in 1883.

" Mr. Goschen, I should observe, is not in any sense of the word a Bimetallist ; that is, he has not as yet in any way declared himself in favour of Bimetallism. He seems indeed to have some hesitation in taking sides, one way or the other. But nothing could be more explicit than his statements as to the increase in the purchasing power of gold, and nothing could be more lucid than his account of the causes that have led to that increase.

" In his address delivered in 1883 he went into this matter in full detail. He showed how, in the years from 1873 to 1883, whilst the annual supply of gold had fallen off to a most notable extent, the demands upon the existing stock of gold in the world, especially from the substitution of a gold currency for a silver currency in Germany and other countries had enormously increased.'

" The facts dealt with by Mr. Goschen in that address are very clearly summed up by Mr. Samuel Smith in the interesting volume from which I have so often quoted.

" ' The gold production,' he says, ' which for some years exceeded 30 millions annually, has fallen to 19 millions a-year ; and the best continental authorities, such as Soetbeer and Laveleye, reckon that more than half that amount is consumed in the arts. It may, therefore, be reckoned that, since 1873, only some 10 millions of gold, on the average, has been available for currency purposes.

" ' But Germany during that period has introduced a gold currency of 80 millions ; the United States . . . has used up 100 millions ; and Italy has drawn some 20 millions

---

[1] *On the Probable Results of an Increase in the Purchasing Power of Gold.* By the Right Hon. G. J. Goschen. M.P., London, 1883. pages 1-3.

for a similar purpose. So that 200 millions have been withdrawn for these special purposes, whereas the whole supply of new gold for coinage has not exceeded, in that time, 130 millions. The balance must have been drawn out of existing stocks. Besides, a steady drain of some 4 millions a-year has gone to India, further depleting the stock in Europe. . . .

" ' While trade and population constantly grow and demand more metallic currency, there is a steadily diminishing quantity to meet it.

" ' If we put the present production of gold at 19 millions a-year, and the requirements of the arts at 8 to 10 millions a-year, while the ordinary Indian demand is 4 millions, there is only left 5 to 7 millions a-year for new coinage, for Europe, America, and the British Colonies.

" ' It will seem to subsequent ages the height of folly that, just at this period, when gold was running short, the chief States of the world decided to close their Mints against silver, and cut off, so to speak one-half the money supply of the world from performing its proper functions. . . .

" ' Had the world continued to use both metals as freely as before, the painful crisis we have passed through would have been much mitigated. But by a suicidal policy, silver was cut off at the very time when it was most needed, and a double burden thrown upon gold just when it was only able to bear half its former burden.

" ' As Bismarck has well said, two men were struggling to lie under a blanket only big enough for one.' '

" It would be a grave omission here not to quote

---

¹ *The Bimetallic Question.* By Samuel Smith, M.P. Essay on *The Sufferings caused by the Appreciation of the Gold Standard*, pages 140, 141.

Mr. Goschen's further remarks as to the inevitable further increase in the value of gold—the result of not merely a continuance, but a growth, of the present exhausting demand upon it.

"Mr. Goschen's treatment of this aspect of the case is all the more valuable from its forestalling a difficulty which is not at all unlikely to occur to those who enter upon the examination of the currency question without being very fully informed upon the nature of financial operations as they are carried but on an extensive scale in the great money markets of the world.

"'If it be true,' says Mr. Goschen, 'that population continually increases, and that there is a certain increase in wealth, an additional amount of circulation will be necessary in order to meet the increased demand, unless there are compensating counter economies by the extension of the cheque system and other methods.

"'Now, on the one hand, you undoubtedly have increased population. Going back thirty years, you may say you have an addition to the population of 50 per cent, including not only the gold-using countries of the old world, but new countries, such as Australia, where the population increases fast.

"'You also have an increase of wealth. Then, again, you require more gold for more transactions. . . .

"'Let us now consider, on the other hand, whether the economies in the use of gold have been so great as the increase in the population, and as the increase in the amount of gold required to liquidate the balance of transactions.

"'Mr. Giffen, in an article . . . printed in the Journal of the Statistical Society for March, 1879, expresses

the opinion that the United Kingdom was thoroughly
'well banked' even 20 years ago, and that there have
been no new devices invented during the last 20 years
which have much economized the use of gold in the
United Kingdom. We have already, I believe, reduced
the use of gold in this country almost to a minimum;
and I am confirmed in this view by the statement that
the total circulation of gold in England increased, according to the estimate of the authorities of the Bank of
England, from £103,000,000 to £124,000,000 between
1870 to 1880.

"'This would mean—and it is a most significant fact
—that in this country, which is so 'well banked,' to use
Mr. Giffen's phrase, £20,000,000 more circulation was
nevertheless required in 1880 than in 1870.

"'What a pull must those £20,000,000 have been on
the total supply of gold, after, or concurrently with, those
other demands to which I have called your attention.

"'As regards England, then, I do not see that there has
been any economy in the use of gold to counterbalance
the increasing demand of the population, nor are we aware
that in France or Germany, or elsewhere, the economies
have been such as to counterbalance the increasing demand
for gold.'" [1]

"And as to the effect of all this upon prices?"

"That was the main topic of Mr. Goschen's address.
"In that address, he makes good by every possible line
of argument that gold has risen, that it is rising, and that,
in all probability, it will continue to rise, in value. He

[1] *On the Probable Results of an Increase in the Purchasing Power of Gold.*
An Address delivered before the Institute of Bankers, April 18th, 1883, by
the Right Hon. Geo. J. Goschen, M.P. London, 1883, pages 7, 8.

explains, moreover, that this increase in the value of gold is the true explanation of the 'fall in prices,' which had become unmistakeably evident even at the time of the delivery of his address, in 1883.

" After working out all this in detail, Mr. Goschen adds the curiously significant remark that 'some writers have appeared to show something approaching to irritation at the view that the situation of gold should have largely influenced prices.' 'I scarcely,' he says, 'know why, unless through *the apprehension that the Bimetallists may utilize the argument.*'

" This, written six years beforehand, forms an instructive commentary on Mr. Giffen's odd change of front.[1]

" And then Mr. Goschen adds :—' I must repeat that, to my mind, the connection between the additional demand for gold and the position of prices, seems as *sound in principle* as I believe it to be *sustained by facts.*'[2]

" Well, no doubt, it is a very natural apprehension, that Bimetallists should utilize an argument, the basis of which is so emphatically certified as not merely 'sustained by facts,' but also as 'sound in principle,' by one of the most eminent practical financiers in England.

" I have already mentioned the proposal that has been made in view of the terribly serious difficulties resulting from the difference of standards between England and India. It has been suggested, as a means of getting over all these difficulties, that the Indian currency should be re-constituted on the basis of a gold standard.

" But this, from the further demand it would make upon the existing stock of gold in the world, would necessarily lead to a further increase in the value of gold, and would

[1] See pages, 65, 66.
[2] *On the Probable Results of an Increase in the Purchasing Power of Gold* By the Right Hon. Geo. J. Goschen, M.P.; London, 1883, page 20.

thereby most seriously aggravate the evils of the present situation throughout the commercial world.

"As Mr. Goschen forcibly expressed it at the Paris Conference of 1878:—'If other States were to carry on a propaganda in favour of a gold standard and of the demonetisation of silver, the Indian Government would be obliged to reconsider its position, and might be forced by events to take measures similar to those taken elsewhere. *In that case the scramble to get rid of silver might provoke one of the gravest crises ever undergone by commerce.*'[1]

"So far, then, for the tendency of gold, in the present monetary arrangements of the commercial world, to increase in value.

"Now, as to the remedy which Bimetallists propose. This, as we have seen, is, to put silver into the standard currency concurrently with gold—by opening the mints for the unlimited coinage of the two metals at a fixed ratio

---

[1] Quoted by Professor Nicholson, in *Money and Monetary Problems*, pages 111, 112.

[2] "There are some who deny this, on the ground that 'money was never so cheap as now,' to use the parlance of the market.

"It is true that *the rate of interest was never lower*, and in that sense the very inaccurate phrase 'cheap money' is quite true. But all monetary authorities know well that the two things are quite distinct.

"The rate [of interest] for the use of capital, and the purchasing power of gold, are wholly different things. The former varies with the state of credit, the activity of trade, &c., and would do so whether the purchasing power of gold were great or small. . .

"Indeed a fall in prices has a tendency to keep down the rate of interest, as it causes much distress, and a want of confidence among the commercial classes ; hence unused capital accumulates, and the curious phenomenon is witnessed of the value of money, *i.e.* its purchasing power, increasing while the rate of interest declines." *The Bimetallist Question.* By Samuel Smith, M.P. *Essay on Gold and Silver and the Depression of Trade*, pages 87, 88.

"The very low rate of interest is a proof of the deadness of trade. Indeed as prices fall, and gold appreciates [that is to say, increases in value], the interest of capital is always low. . . . What is called 'cheap money,' or a low rate of interest, is usually coexistent with an increased purchasing power in the standard of value ; and money accumulates in banks, because the commercial public cannot use it profitably." *Ibid., Answers to Questions on Currency and Prices*, page 109.

of value, and making both the gold and silver coinage 'legal tender'[1] to any amount.[2]

"Their main point is that the introduction of silver in this way into the standard coinage would check the tendency of money to 'appreciate,' or increase in value. It manifestly would tend to check that tendency by broadening the base on which the monetary system stands.

"Statisticians tell us that the quantity of coined gold in the world amounts to about £800,000,000 sterling, and the quantity of coined silver to about £700,000,000. The precise figures, in such a case as this, are not of very great consequence. For we may take it, at all events, that the amounts are something about those mentioned. Plainly, the causes that tend to affect the value of either of the two precious metals would have a far less disturbing effect upon a standard of value composed of the two metals, conjointly, to the value of 1,500 millions sterling, than it would have upon a currency of only half the amount.

"Then, furthermore, it is to be remembered that this enlarged currency would consist, not of one metal, but of two.

"It is, no doubt, possible that the tendencies of the two metals to fluctuate in value[3] may coincide in direction and in degree. But it is in the highest degree improbable that this will always, or even frequently, occur. Whilst the value of one metal, under the operation of the law of supply and demand, tends to go up, the tendency of the other is quite as likely to be downward. Or, if both tend to move in the same direction, all the probabilities are that their respective tendencies will differ in degree, and the difference is by no means unlikely to be a very notable one. So each will serve, at all events in some degree, to counteract the other.[4]

---

[1] See page 22, *footnote* 1.   [2] See page 28.   [3] See pages 14, 15.
[4] 'I cannot conceive how anyone who has studied this question can doubt

" Professor Jevons—though he was not a Bimetallist [1]— gives an admirable example of the effect produced by the introduction of a second metal into the standard currency, in checking the tendency to fluctuations in value.

" He gives the example of two reservoirs of water, each subject to independent variations of supply and demand. In the absence of any connecting pipe, the level of the water in each reservoir will be subject to its own fluctuations only. But if we open a connection, the water in both will assume a certain mean level, and the effects of any excessive supply or demand will be distributed over the whole area of both reservoirs.

" ' The mass of the metals,' he says, ' gold and silver, circulating in Western Europe in late years, is exactly represented by the water in these reservoirs, and the

that a currency formed of two metals would be less liable to violent changes of value than the existing Monometallic currency." Speech of the Right Hon. A. J. Balfour in the House of Commons, on April 18th, 1890. See Hansard, 3rd Series, vol. 343, pp. 806, 7.

[1] If I were to put it rather in this way, that Professor Jevons' brilliant career was cut short by its untimely end before he had fully come round, as so many other leading economists have come round, from Monometallism to Bimetallism, the expression would not be without justification.

Speaking of Professor Jevons, Mr. Barclay (*The Silver Question and the Gold Question*, Introduction, pages 6, 7) says—and the quotation is of special appropriateness here:—

" Though opposing the views which it is the object of these pages to advocate, his writings have done much to establish them, more especially the demonstration he has made as to *the smaller variation in the value of money* in relation to commodities, *under a double standard of gold and silver, than of gold alone.*

" Time, I believe, with him might have wrought further change, for we must bear in mind that the idea that gold was the only standard which civilised nations should have, was, 17 or 18 years ago, almost universally entertained. It was a cherished dream of perfection in money which the economists of that time held dear. . .

" Many of those now known as Bimetallists at one time shared the same views ; and I think it is not assuming too much to believe that the attitude, as ' of travellers lost in a fog, waiting till the air becomes clear'—which Jevons advocated in one of his latest papers on the subject—might, in the fuller light which experience is throwing upon the question, have resulted in his making a further advance towards what Wolowski with his clearer perception so early discerned as the truth."

As to all this, see also pages 97 and 98 of this Pamphlet.

connecting pipe is the law of the 7th Germinal, an XI. [the law establishing Bimetallism in France in 1803],[1] which enables one metal to take the place of the other as an unlimited legal tender.'

"Mr. Samuel Smith gives another illustration. He takes the case of a kite. If the currency consists of gold only, then we have a kite without a tail, blown hither and thither by every wind. If we have a combination of gold and silver, linked together in a monetary system at a fixed ratio of value, then we have a kite with a heavy tail attached to it and steadying it."

"But is it really possible at this time of day, by any State regulation, to fix the price of silver or of anything else? Will not the price of any precious metal, in spite of artificial restriction, find its level in the market[2] under the law of supply and demand?"

"That is the stock fallacy of the Monometallists, I mean the Monometallists of the older, but now rapidly dwindling, school.

"Of course, supply and demand will regulate all prices— the price of silver or gold, as well as of everything else. But this precisely is the reason why Bimetallism is an effective means of keeping gold and silver at a fixed ratio of value in the bullion markets of the world.

"Legislation cannot directly give value to a thing, *but it can set up a demand*[3] *which is one of the factors of value.*

"The opening of a sufficient number of mints for what practically amounts to the purchase of silver at a certain price relative to gold, establishes a constant demand for

---

[1] See pages 27, 28.   [2] See pages 14, 15.   [3] See pages 16, 17.

silver at that price.[1] So long as Bimetallism was upheld in the French and other mints, the ratio was kept steady.

" It was kept steady, too, not in contravention of the law of supply and demand, but precisely because of the operation of that law. The State arrangement[2] for the unrestricted coinage of both metals in those mints at the fixed ratio of $15\frac{1}{2}$ of silver to 1 of gold, was, in fact, the mainspring of the working of the law of supply and demand in the case.

" The arrangement that was in operation in the various mints *constituted a permanent demand for each of the two precious metals at that fixed ratio between the mint values of the two.* Those who had silver anywhere to dispose of would not part with 18 or 20 ounces of it for an ounce of gold, when by sending their silver to a public mint they could get as good a price for $15\frac{1}{2}$ ounces.[3]

" Then, moreover, Bimetallists call attention to a series of undoubtedly striking facts in connection with all this.

" During a long period of years preceding 1873, almost every kind of disturbance that could by any possibility have interfered with the relative value of gold and silver occurred in the monetary world. Still, throughout it all, the relative value of the two stood practically unchanged.[4]

" ' The ratio of $15\frac{1}{2}$ to 1,' says Mr. Samuel Smith,

---

[1] " For my part, I have always held, and on that point I have understood I am on the side of Bimetallists, that the question of the value of silver and gold was not a simple question of natural supply and demand: and that position on my part, I dare say, is looked upon as a heresy by the extreme disciples of the Monometallist school.

" I think it cannot be denied that Government action in various States has had an enormous effect on the relative value of silver and gold. The action of the Latin Union, the action of Germany, the displacement of silver and the enthronement of gold in its place in many countries, have had an immense effect in producing the changes which the Bimetallists deplore and attempt to remedy." Speech of the Right Hon. George J. Goschen in the Town Hall, Manchester, November 17th, 1887.

[2] See page 28.   [3] See pages 31-33.   [4] See pages 60-62.

existed during a long period, when silver was annually produced to three or four times the value of gold, and during another long period when gold was annually produced to three or four times the value of silver.

" ' It was equally unaffected by the great increase in the cost of producing silver during the Civil Wars in South America, which closed the richest silver mines, and by the extraordinary decrease in the cost of producing gold, when the rich mines of Australia and California were first discovered.

" ' It was equally unaffected by the entire cessation of the great Eastern demand for silver which happened once or twice in the earlier part of the century, or by the extraordinary demand which set in during the time of the Cotton Famine.

" ' Neither was it affected by the vast displacements of specie that occurred in many countries—such as the United States of America, Italy, Austria, &c—caused by war, or national bankruptcy, when inconvertible paper expelled metallic money.

" ' It may be asserted, in brief, that every possible convulsion occurred in the monetary world during the first three-quarters of this century, and yet the tie between gold and silver was not broken.

" ' So long as the French Mint was open to coin either of them to an unlimited extent, and as full legal tender, it mattered not whether the yield of gold was two millions a-year, or thirty millions ; whether the yield of silver was six, or sixteen millions ; whether the miners in Australia were extracting gold at a cost of £1 per ounce, or the miners in Nevada were producing silver at 1s. 6d. per ounce.'

' *The Bimetallic Question.* By Samuel Smith, M.P. London, 1887
Essay on Bimetallic Money, page 11.

"Between 1848 and 1870, *the stock of gold money in the world, according to trustworthy estimates, increased by nearly* 90 *per cent*, whilst *the quantity of silver money in the world increased by only* 10 *per cent*. But still, under the natural operation of the Bimetallic system of France and other countries, *the relative value* of gold and silver *stood practically unchanged*."

" That, as we now know, is no longer the case ? "

" Unfortunately for many interests, it is not. The Royal Commission of 1887 gives a table which shows that the annual average price of silver on the London market, from 1833 to 1872, never was lower than 4*s*. 10¾*d*. per ounce, and never was higher than 5*s*. 2¾*d*.—showing a variation only of 4*d*. The same table shows how different the case has been since 1873. Between 1873 and 1887 the price ranged from 4*s*. 11¼*d*. down to 3*s*. 6*d*.—showing a variation of 1*s*. 5¾*d*., as against an extreme variation of only 4*d*. in the former period." ₁

" But what about the Monometallist members of the Commission ? Do they admit that the relative values of gold and silver can be fixed by State regulations ? "

" Certainly. In the earlier stages of the controversy about Bimetallism, the question whether the relative value of gold and silver could be so fixed was looked upon as one of the great test questions between Monometallists and Bimetallists.

" Monometallists tried to make out that the relative value of gold and silver was kept steady down to 1873

¹ See also pages 60-62.

—not by the State arrangement then in force in France and the other countries of the Latin Union—but by a whole complicated series of independent causes, all happening to work in the right direction to bring about this happy result.'

" But, as Mr. Samuel Smith has pointedly expressed it. these attempted explanations of the Monometallists ' remind one of nothing so much as the hopeless attempts of the ancient astronomers to explain the movements of the heavenly bodies on the theory that the earth was the centre of the universe.' ²

" That day, however, is past. Leading Monometallists have long since found themselves forced to acknowledge that on this vital point the Bimetallists were right.

" Here. for instance, are two important passages from the Report of the Royal Commission.

" I take the first from that portion of the Report which is signed unanimously by the 12 members of the Commission,³ Monometallists and Bimetallists alike.

" After setting forth a number of figures illustrative of

---

¹ " I am sometimes astonished at the obstinate refusal of many people to learn from the clearest experience.

" Nobody can doubt that there was. broadly speaking, this par of exchange for a very long period of time. Nobody can doubt that during that time there was a Bimetallic system existing in France and in other Latin Unions. Nevertheless there are some people who say the two facts, both of which must be admitted. have no cause or connection with each other, and that by a series of extraordinary coincidences it did so happen that the par of exchange was maintained, and not to the existence of the Bimetallic system.

" They construct a huge scaffolding of coincidences. The whole thing is to be explained, not by one general principle applicable to the whole phenomena, but by a series of hypotheses, each of them extravagant. and still more extravagant when taken together : and thus a fact that we can explain by a stroke of the pen is accounted for." Speech of the Right Hon. A. J. Balfour, M.P., at the Town Hall, Manchester, 27th October, 1892. London and Manchester. 1892, page 27.

² The Bimetallist Question. By Samuel Smith, M.P. London, 1877 Essay on Bimetallic Money, page 10.

³ See page 38.

the notable unsteadiness of the price of silver in recent years—the unsteadiness, that is to say, of the 'gold price of silver, or, in other words, the relative value of the two metals—the Report continues as follows:—

" ' The explanation commonly offered of those constant variations in the silver market is, that the rise or depression of the price of silver depends upon the briskness or slackness of the demand, for the purpose of remittance to silver-using countries, and that the price is largely affected by the amount of the bills sold from time to time by the Secretary of State for India . . .

" ' But these causes were, as far as can be seen, operating prior to 1873, as well as subsequent to that date, and yet the silver market did not display the sensitiveness to those influences, day by day, and month to month, which it now does.

" ' These considerations seem to suggest the existence of some steadying influence in former periods, which has now been removed, and which has left the silver market subject to the free influence of causes, the full effect of which was previously kept in check.'[1]

"Then, in reference to the Bimetallic arrangement maintained in France and the other countries mentioned, the Commissioners go on to say:—

" ' The question therefore forces itself upon us:—Is there any circumstance, calculated to affect the relation of silver to gold, which distinguishes the latter period from the earlier?

" ' Now, undoubtedly, the date which forms the dividing line between an epoch of approximate fixity in the relative value of gold and silver, and one of marked instability, is

[1] *Report of the Gold and Silver Commission.* 1888. Part I. nn. 191, 192.

the year when the Bimetallic system which had previously been in force in the Latin Union ceased to be in full operation, and *we are irresistibly led to the conclusion* that the operation of that system, established as it was in countries the population and commerce of which were considerable, exerted a material influence upon the relative value of the two metals.

" ' So long as that system was in force we think that, notwithstanding the changes in the production and use of the precious metals, *it kept the market price of silver approximately*[1] *steady* at the ratio of 15½ to 1. . .'

" Not satisfied with all this, the Commissioners go on to refute the chief arguments relied upon by leading opponents of Bimetallism in support of their view that the existence of that legal ratio in the States of the Latin Union could not operate so as to keep the price of silver steady in the London and other markets.

" Here is how they put it :—

" ' Nor does it appear to us as *a priori* unreasonable to suppose that the existence in the Latin Union of a Bimetallic system with a ratio of 15½ to 1 fixed between the two metals should have been capable of keeping the market price of silver steady at approximately[2] that ratio.

" ' The view that it could only affect the market price to the extent to which there was a demand for it for currency purposes in the Latin Union, or to which it was actually taken to the mints of those countries, is, we think, fallacious.

" ' The fact that *the owner of silver could, in the last resort, take it to those mints*, and have it converted into coin which would purchase commodities at the ratio of 15½

---

[1] See page 33, *footnote*.   [2] *Ibid*.

of silver to 1 of gold, would, in our opinion, be likely to affect the price of silver in the market generally, whoever the purchaser, and for whatever country it was destined. It would *enable the seller to stand out for a price approximating to the legal ratio,* and would tend to keep the market steady at about that point.'[1]

" The Commissioners then proceed to dispose of another argument that had been pressed upon them :—

" ' It has been urged that during the earlier of the two periods which we have been contrasting [the periods preceding and following the date of the change made in 1873], the conditions which existed from time to time were favourable to the maintenance of the legal ratio. . . .

" ' But we do not think this affords an adequate solution of the problem, without taking into account the existence of the Bimetallic system. It may be true that the circumstances referred to were conditions which helped to make the Bimetallic system operative. But, as we observed before, circumstances and conditions of a like nature have been more or less operative both before and since 1873, and yet the effect on the relative value of the two metals has been very different.'[2]

" I have quoted all this from that portion of the Report which, as I have said, represents the unanimous view of the 12 members of the Royal Commission, Monometallists and Bimetallists alike.

" Then in the special Report drawn up by the 6 Monometallist members of that Commission, the following important passage occurs. It is signed, without qualification or reserve, by 4 out of the 6 :—

[1] *Report of the Gold and Silver Commission*, 1888. Part 1, nn. 192, 193.
[2] *Ibid.*, n. 194.

" ' We think that, on any conditions fairly to be contemplated in the future, so far as we can forecast them from the experience of the past, a stable ratio might be maintained if the nations we have alluded to [the United Kingdom, Germany, the United States, and the Latin Union] were to accept and strictly adhere to Bimetallism at the suggested ratio.

" ' We think that if, in all these countries, gold and silver could be freely coined, and thus become exchangeable against commodities at the fixed rates, *the market value of silver as measured by gold would conform to that ratio, and not vary to any material extent.*

" ' We need not enter upon a detailed explanation of our reasons for entertaining this view, since they will be gathered from what we have already stated . . . and will be seen to result, in our judgment, *as well from a priori reasoning as from the experience of the last half century.*'[1]

" It would seem, indeed, impossible to maintain any other view.

" Two of the six Monometallist members of the Commission did not wish to endorse this particular portion of the Report drawn up by their Monometallist colleagues. But they cannot be said to have dissented very strongly from it. In the Note appended by them to the Report, they merely express a 'doubt' upon the matter. Practically, then, we may take it that the point is no longer open to serious controversy.

" Mr. Giffen, indeed, the eminent official statistician of the Board of Trade, has been carried away by the ardour of his Monometallism into misrepresenting, to a **very**

<hr>

[1] *Royal Commission on Gold and Silver*, 1888, Report, part ii., n. 107.'

serious extent, the action of the two Commissioners in question. He says they ‘dissented’ from this part of the Report, and expressed their ‘conviction’ that such a ratio could not be maintained permanently.[1]

“As a matter of fact, however, the words of the Note appended by the two Commissioners in question are merely these :—‘we *doubt* whether any given ratio could be permanently maintained.’[2]

“This may be a convenient place to interpose a remark or two upon the attitude taken up towards Bimetallism and Bimetallists by Mr. Giffen.

“Mr. Giffen’s volume upon the subject is, from first to last, a continuous indictment of Bimetallism and of those who have written in advocacy of it—a good deal of the indictment being expressed in language that would be of singular appropriateness if applied to a number of lunatics and to their crazy hallucinations.

“That I may not seem to be overstating this matter, I ought, perhaps, to give a few illustrations of the style in which the views and the arguments of even leading exponents of Bimetallism, men of European reputation, such as Emile de Laveleye and others, are freely spoken of by Mr. Giffen:—

“‘The whole character of their arguments is essentially tainted and unsound.’[3] ‘M. de Laveleye intervened and set forth the ordinary ideas of the currency faddist.’[4] ‘The Bimetallist argument is tainted, and this accounts very much, I believe, for the extreme disgust and dislike, . . . the detestation of men of sense.’[5] ‘If economists like Mr. Bagehot can hardly be brought to overcome

[1] *The Case against Bimetallism*, by Robert Giffen : London, 1892, page 117.
[2] *Royal Commission on Gold and Silver*, 1888. Final Report, pages 93, 94.
[3] *The Case against Bimetallism*, by Robert Giffen, page 2.
[4] *Ibid*, page 5.   [5] *Ibid.*, page 17.

their disgust at the argument for Bimetallism, so as to turn aside even to discuss it, they are surely not without excuse. Mathematicians do not stop to argue with squarers of the circle, or with reasoners that the earth is flat.' [1] 'The extravagance and intemperance of idea among Bimetallists regarding money and currency, this extravagance and intemperance being characteristic of the currency faddist.' [2] 'Sismondi is obviously no authority on this question, not having studied it at all ; . . such as he is, however, Sismondi is still the leading authority, so far as I know, for the Bimetallic view.' [3] 'That folly.' [4]

" With Mr. Giffen, the impossibility of controlling, by means of a legal ratio, the relative value of gold and silver, is an established scientific truth.

" As might be expected, then, from the passages I have just quoted from his writings, he uses somewhat strong language in reference to the action of the members of the Royal Commission upon this important point. His indignation, of course, is directed with special energy against those members of the Commission who, as Monometallists, were specially charged with the defence of the Monometallist position at all points, but who, nevertheless, expressed their full concurrence in the view of their Bimetallist colleagues, that the old notion of the impossibility of fixing the relative value of gold and silver had to be abandoned as untenable.

" He pronounces, in fact, against them a sentence of excommunication from the Monometallist body. He describes them as ' the *so-called Monometallic* section ' of the Commission, which section he says ' should perhaps be preferably called the *non-Bimetallic section.*' [5]

[1] *The Case against Bimetallism*, by Robert Giffen : London, 1892, page 37.
[2] *Ibid.*, page 7. [3] *Ibid.*, page 113. [4] *Ibid.*, page 134, 5. [5] *Ibid.*, page 7.

"Then we have such expressions as, 'the remarkable aberration of the Gold and Silver Commission;'[1] the views of inconvertible paper faddists, endorsed,' but 'accidentally', by Royal Commissioners;'[2] the 'persistence' of the Royal Commissioners in 'error;'[3] overlooking 'what was staring them in the face,'[4] and so on.

"He complains of it too as 'a scandal of the first magnitude' that 'men of light and leading in other respects should have talked seriously, even if only for a moment, of any such thing even as the possibility of a fixed price between gold and silver.'[5]   It seems that some of the members of the Royal Commission resented, very naturally indeed, the use of such a phrase, 'a scandal of the first magnitude,' as applied to what they had done.   Then, by way, as it were, of mending matters, Mr. Giffen, in republishing his paper in which the offensive expression occurs, has added a foot-note pointing out that 'it is obvious that in the passage there is no reference to the Royal Commission or its members.'[6]

"Now, undoubtedly, the thing so roundly denounced by Mr. Giffen's as 'a scandal of the first magnitude' was the very thing that was done by those Monometallist members of the Royal Commission.   His point, then, seems to be that, inasmuch as only 'men of light and leading' were referred to in his criticism, no one, except perhaps the Royal Commissioners themselves, could suppose there was any reference to them in the insulting observation. At all events, as to the obnoxious phrase, Mr. Giffen refuses to withdraw it or to modify it.

"But the question of the possibility of maintaining an

---

[1] *The Case against Bimetallism.* By Robert Giffen : London. 1892, page 139.
[2] *Ibid.*, page 140.   [3] *Ibid.*, page 149.   [4] *Ibid.*, page 151.
[5] *Ibid.*, page 131.   [6] *Ibid.*, page 131.

approximately steady ratio of values between the two precious metals is not to be decided by mere vehemence of language. The Report of the Royal Commission points out, with manifest truth, that it is a question practically decided by ' the experience of the last half century.' [1]

" It seems impossible, for instance, to evade the force of the following facts.

" First, from 1803 to 1873, whilst the Bimetallist arrangements of France were in force, the market prices of gold and silver, ea ch year, kept so close to the French currency value of $15\frac{1}{2}$ to 1, that they never oscillated so far even as 16 to 1 on the one side, or 15 to 1 on the other.

" But then, in the year 1874, the year after the change in the French system, the market ratio at once rose to over 16 to 1. In 1876, 1877, and 1878, it was over 17 to 1. From 1879 to 1884, it was over 18 to 1. In 1885 it was over 19 to 1.

" Then, with certain fluctuations, it still kept on rising. On the 24th of September of the present year, 1892, the latest date for which I have seen a return, it was about 24 to 1."

" The former steadiness, then, was the result of the arrangements in operation at the French and other Mints? "

" Yes : that is to say, it was the result of the demand [2] set up for each of the two metals at the relative value of $15\frac{1}{2}$ to 1. But there is a point of great importance to be mentioned here. It may be useful to mention it, to guard against a possible misconception.

" What was fixed by the action of France and

[1] See page 83. [2] See pages 75, 76.

the other countries of the Latin Union was *the ratio of the values of gold and silver*, compared one with another.

"Fixing the relative value of the two metals, that is, the ratio between the values of the two parts out of which the whole monetary stock of the world is made up, is quite a different thing from fixing the value of money, that is to say, the purchasing power of money as regards commodities.

"It is quite consistent with the maintenance of a fixed proportion of value between the two metals which go to make up the metallic currency, that the value of the currency itself, taken as a whole, should be liable to fluctuations.[1] I have already mentioned that the maintenance of an absolutely invariable standard of value—whether consisting of one metal, or of two metals linked together in a fixed ratio of value to one another—is a matter of practical impossibility.[2] The value of money, that is to say, the value of the whole stock of coined metal must, like the value of everything that is marketable, be regulated by the law of supply and demand.

"But whilst the purchasing power of the whole stock of the money of the world may so vary, the relative value of the two portions of it, that portion of it which is in gold, and that portion of it which is in silver, may be kept in the same proportion towards each other,

---

[1] " I shall not ask you to believe that even with Bimetallism you are certain to escape altogether from a gradual [increase in the value] of the standard when you come to compare a long term of years.

" But what I do maintain is, that with the two metals in full use, the general level of prices will be *much more steady*, and any increase in the value] of the double standard will be *much more gradual*, than in the opposite case." Nicholson. *Money and Monetary Problems*. page 233.

[2] See page 15.

so that, although the number, whether of sovereigns or of rupees, required for purchasing a given quantity of other marketable goods,[1] may sometimes be greater and sometimes less, the same number of sovereigns shall always practically be worth the same number of rupees.[2] That is the first advantage secured by a Bimetallist system.

"Then there is another point. Although an absolutely invariable standard of value is practically unattainable by legislation,[3] it is plain that a much higher degree of steadiness of value in the monetary standard may be attained by making that standard consist of the two metals, gold and silver, conjointly, than if it consisted of either of those metals alone. Obviously the combination of the two metals makes up a currency far less liable to be affected by whatever fluctuations may occur, than any currency composed of one or the other metal alone.[1]

"In that way, the Bimetallic system of France and of the other countries of the Latin Union, secured for those countries—and indirectly for the rest of the commercial world[5]—not merely a fixed ratio of value as between gold and silver, but also, in large measure, a monetary standard as free from fluctuations in value as is practically possible of attainment.

"Let us look back to Professor Jevons' illustration, the two reservoirs with the connecting pipe between them.[6] When there is a difference between the total inflow and the total outflow—taking both reservoirs into account—no possible freedom of connection between the reservoirs can hinder the common level from being affected

---

[1] See pages 14, 15.
[2] See pages 24, 25.
[3] See page 15.
[4] See pages 73-75.
[5] See pages 31-33.
[6] See page 74.

by that difference. But the effect of the connection between the two is to keep the fluctuations of the common level in both reservoirs as free from fluctuations as is consistent with the continuance of an inflow and of an outflow, both constantly varying."

"In that way, then, Bimetallism checks the tendency to variation in the value of the monetary standard?"

"Yes; it checks that tendency; but we must remember that it only checks it. The check which it applies is, indeed, a very notable, a very substantial one. But the tendency to variation in value cannot be altogether eliminated.[1]

"As Mr. Samuel Smith explains this point, '*What the law cannot fix is the purchasing power of the precious metals in relation to other commodities.*

"'Suppose, for argument sake, that the joint production of gold and silver, which is now[2] about 33 millions annually, were to become 100 millions, we should find a rapid rise in money prices; in other words, a diminution in the purchasing power of money.

"'But *what the law can do is to prevent fluctuations in value as between gold and silver*, by making them both legal tender at a definite rate. . . .

"'As stability of value is one of the most necessary qualities of money, . . . it is better to confine fluctuations to the mass of gold and silver combined, than let each metal fluctuate separately.

"'Gold alone has varied within this century from an annual production of £3,000,000 to £30,000,000, or tenfold.

[1] See page 15.   [2] This was written in 1876.

But gold and silver combined have only varied from about £10,000,000 to £40,000,000, or fourfold—hence the joint metal forms a more stable mass than gold alone.'

" Here is where Mr. Smith brings in the comparison I have already mentioned ' :—' It is like a kite with a heavy tail to it, which prevents the kite from swaying to and fro ; whereas gold alone is a kite without a tail which obeys every gust more readily.'

" Stability of value in the monetary standard of value is, of course, of very great importance.[2] But the importance of it is sometimes overlooked. In view of this aspect of the case, some newspaper disquisitions on the currency question are amusing. Here, for instance, is a characteristic specimen :—

' If two sovereigns at the present value of gold have the same purchasing power which three sovereigns used to have, the obvious result is that two sovereigns will serve just as well as three.

' Thus by natural causes there comes an economy of gold to the precise extent to which there exists a need for it.

' The balance is self-adjusting.' [3]

" That, of course, would be perfectly true if money were merely a medium of exchange, to be employed in buying and selling, the transactions moreover being for immediate cash. But money, as we have already seen, has another and most important function. It forms—to use Mr. Balfour's expressive words—the 'record of obligations extending over long periods of time.' [4]

" It is in view of this important function of money—a function which the writer of the curious disquisition I have

---

[1] See page 75. [2] See pages 45-56.
[3] *The Times*, 12th March, 1886, quoted in *The Silver Question in its Social Aspect*. By Hermann Schmidt. London, 1886. page 17.
[4] See page 52.

just quoted, would seem never to have heard of,—that
stability of value, in so far as it is attainable,[1] is one of the
first requirements of a monetary standard."[2]

" Then what do the Monometallists say to all this ? "

" Their position in reference to the practical aspects of
the case is indeed not easy to define. I have already
pointed out how they have been driven back from one line
of defence to another.[3] So far as I have been able to make
out, there are not many of them now who do not admit, to
the full, the existence of the evils I have spoken of, and who
do not admit, moreover, that those evils are mainly, if not
exclusively, the result of an increase in the value of gold.
But then, as regards the remedy for it all, their position seems to be that of men who will merely sit by,
with folded arms, and do nothing.

" Mr. Giffen, indeed, at the end of the statistical paper
from which I have quoted his explicit and emphatic statement as to the notable and still increasing rise in the value
of gold,[4] suggested a remedy for at all events one set of the
evils that result from the present state of affairs—those that
are involved in the unfitness of our gold standard as a measure
of obligation in the case of payments extending over long
periods, such as a term of years. The suggestion was that,
instead of working on the basis of any metallic standard—
whether consisting of one metal or of two—recourse should
be had to the device known as a 'tabular' standard of
value.

" Mr. Giffen, indeed, seems to have given up as hopeless
the possibility of constructing any satisfactory or equitable

---

[1] See page 15.
[2] See pages 45-56.
[3] See pages 56, 57.
[4] See pages 57-65.

system on the basis of specifying, in money, the amounts of payments to be made.

"Here is how he stated his view :—

"'Is there anything to be done by Governments [to provide against the effects of the appreciation of gold], is a question which will naturally arise . . .

"'The only suggestion I would make is of a statistical kind.

"'All these difficulties seem to me to suggest the expediency of further scientific study . . of the theory and practice of index numbers,[1] which supply a means of providing for deferred payments *by substituting a different currency for money*, as is done by the corn averages for tithe and by corn rents generally.[2]

---

[1] See pages 58-64.

[2] "In the year 1866, and again in 1870, differences arose between Captain Nolan [now Colonel Nolan, M.P.] and some tenants whom he had evicted in the County Galway. Captain Nolan proposed that the matter in dispute should be left to the arbitration of any three men whom the tenants would name or be satisfied with.

"All parties quickly agreed to the appointment of the following gentlemen as arbitrators: Sir John Gray, M.P., Father Lavelle, and Mr. A. M. Sullivan.

"After several days' deliberations, having held a public court on the spot, examined witnesses, and thoroughly investigated all the circumstances connected with the case, the arbitrators made an award acquitting Captain Nolan of all personal blame, though holding him legally accountable for the acts of his agents, and ordering that certain of the tenants who had been evicted should be restored to their old homesteads or placed in possession of new ones on terms laid down in the award.

"These terms were that Captain Nolan should grant to the tenants such a lease as the arbitrators would frame or approve of.

"The result was the Portacarron Lease. This document seems to have been framed, not with a view merely of adjusting the relations between Captain Nolan and his tenantry, but with the design, apparently, of indicating certain lines within which it might, in the future, be possible to formulate a scheme or plan for dealing with the whole question of the tenure of land in Ireland.

"Term : 10,000 years.

"Rent : initial rent by valuation ; to be *increasable or decreasable* at the end of every ten years, according as the past ten years' *average price of ten articles of farm produce rose or fell*, as compared with the price of them at the date of the lease, endorsed on the back of the document . . ." *The Parliamentary History of the Irish Land Question*. By R. Barry O'Brien. (3rd Edition), London, 1880, pages 194, 5.

"The principal portions of the "Portacarron Lease" are quoted at

" ' If we cannot invent a money that will be stable over generations, may it not be possible to devise a substitute by which the deferred payments will themselves change with the changing value measured by some other standard ? . . .

" ' This last suggestion can hardly be expected to be a very popular one at present, while, as yet, index numbers are hardly known to the public. It is *remote enough from any practical issues*. But . . knowledge is always useful, and a clear insight into what is going on, and what is fairly to be anticipated, may both prevent panic and enable business people to make sensible arrangements in their provisions for the future which otherwise they would not think of.

" ' In documents charging estates, for instance, lawyers might have been able to save their clients much embarrassment, in charging *a percentage of net rental* only, or a sum to be varied by another measure, as the tithe is varied, instead of a fixed and unchangeable sum in money[1] . . .

" ' Business men must consider carefully the effect of engagements to pay money at distant dates.

" ' Many mischiefs might have been avoided if all concerned had realised, 10 or 15 years ago, what was likely to happen in money,[2] and good will now be done if possibilities are kept steadily in view.' " [3]

" The idea of such a ' tabular standard ' of value is not a new one. It is discussed by many writers on the currency question.

" If it were to be worked out in practice, the first requisite would be the appointment of a permanent

length in an Appendix to Mr. Barry O'Brien's interesting and valuable volume (*Ibid.*, pages 215. 18.)

[1] But, of course, if that plan had been adopted, the borrower could hardly have obtained the requisite loan except at a higher rate of interest.

[2] See pages 97 and 98.

[3] *Recent Changes in Prices and Incomes Compared.* By Robt. Giffen : London, 1888, pages 54, 55.

Government Commission, invested with a kind of judicial power. The officers of the Commission would collect the current prices of commodities in all the principal markets of the Kingdom, and by a system of calculation would compute from the data so collected the variations in the purchasing power of gold.

" The decisions of the Commission would then be published at stated intervals, say, monthly ; and all payments would be adjusted in accordance with them.

" Thus, suppose that a debt of £100 was incurred upon the 1st of July, 1875, and was to be paid back on the 1st of July, 1878 ; if the Commission had decided in June, 1878, that the value of gold had fallen in the ratio of 106 to 100 in the intervening years, then the creditor would claim an increase of 6 per cent in the nominal amount of the debt." [1]

" But, plainly, the introduction of such a system would lead to so much complexity in the relations of debtor and creditor that the proposal may well be regarded—to use Mr. Giffen's expression[2]—as 'remote enough from any practical issues.'

" Another suggestion that has been put forward from the Monometallist side is, that the disturbing effects of the increase in the value of gold might be avoided by diminishing the quantity of gold in the sovereign, the quantity of gold being diminished in proportion to the increase in its value.

" Thus, for instance, new sovereigns might now be issued containing about two-thirds of the weight[3] of gold contained in the sovereign as hitherto issued ; next year,

---

[1] See, for instance, Professor Nicholson's *Money and Monetary Problems*: Edinburgh and London, 1888, pages 31, 37, and 298, 331.
[2] See page 94.
[3] See Mr. Balfour's statement, quoted on page 52.

in case the increase in the value of gold continued, there might be a new issue of sovereigns with a proportionately smaller amount of gold ; and so on.[1]

" This, no doubt, if it could be worked out in practice, would meet some of the difficulties of the present situation.   It would at once, for example, give equitable relief to the Irish tenants and tenant-purchasers who are now weighed down by the obligation of making annual payments[2] which, though nominally fixed in amount, really constitute a constantly and indefinitely increasing burden.[3]

" But the plan is wholly impracticable.   One obvious and decisive objection in the way of its adoption is the inextricable confusion that should of necessity result from the difference of value between the sovereigns of the various successive issues, all, as we must assume, being in circulation together.

" The chief importance, indeed, of the suggestion of such an expedient lies in the distinct recognition which it implies of the existence and of the seriousness of the evils resulting from the Monometallic system of currency with its standard of ever-increasing value.

" But, then, the practical question remains, Is nothing to be done ?

" The existence of the evils resulting from the present system can no longer be denied.

" Of the Monometallists it may be said that, whilst fully and frankly admitting the existence of those evils, they have no practical remedy to suggest.   They are satisfied to hold on by the dog-in-the-manger policy of hindering even a trial being given to the remedy proposed by the Bimetallists.

---

[1] See pages 14-19.   [2] See pages 2, 3, 8, 10.
[3] See pages 9-12 ; 45, 46.

" The Bimetallists, on the other hand, have a remedy to propose, and what they propose is nothing new, nothing that has not been tested by long experience. The currency arrangements which they recommend were, as we have seen,[1] in full operation in Europe down to the year 1873.

" In connection with Mr. Giffen's remark that 'many mischiefs might have been avoided if all concerned had realised, 10 or 15 years ago, what was likely to happen in money,'[2] it cannot be out of place to take note of an instructive difference between Monometallists and Bimetallists in reference to this matter of foresight as to the increase in the value of gold, and the evils inevitably resulting from it.

" Whilst the fullest and most distinct warning of all this was given from the Bimetallist side, it was only with extreme difficulty, and not indeed until the Bimetallist predictions had been unmistakeably verified by events, that, with very few exceptions, Monometallists could be brought to realise that any mischief was being done.

" The classic prediction in this matter is that of the French economist, M. Ernest Seyd. So far back as 1871, two years before the calamitous success of the doctrinaire crusade against the maintenance of the Bimetallist system as it was then in operation in France, M. Seyd used the following remarkable words :—

" ' It is a great mistake to suppose that the adoption of the gold [standard of value], by other States besides England,[3] will be beneficial. It will only lead to *the destruction of the monetary equilibrium hitherto existing*, and cause *a fall in the value of silver* from which England's

---

[1] See pages 27, 28.   [2] See page 94.
[3] See pages 31, 32.

trade[1] and the Indian silver valuations[2] will suffer more than all other interests, grievous as the general decline of prosperity all over the world will be.'[3]

" Then comes a singularly noteworthy passage :—

" ' The strong doctrinarianism existing in England as regards the gold valuation is so blind, that, when the time of depression sets in, there will be this special feature :—

" ' The economical authorities of the country will refuse to listen to the cause here foreshadowed : every possible attempt will be made to prove that the decline of commerce is due to all sorts of causes and irreconcileable matters : the workman and his strikes will be the first convenient target ; then 'speculating' and 'overtrading' will have their turn ; . . . many other allegations will be made, totally irrelevant to the real issue, but satisfactory to the moralizing tendency of financial writers.' [4]

" Unfortunately for so many interests, the warning so clearly given by M. Ernest Seyd was disregarded, just as similar warnings as to the disasters that must follow from an obstinate persistence in the mistaken policy adopted in 1873 are being disregarded now."

" But an International Congress is now being assembled for the discussion of the question in all its bearings ? "

" Yes, at Brussels. It is attended by representatives of no fewer than twenty Governments or States. But there are not many in Ireland, I dare say, even of those most directly interested, who have the faintest idea that the question under deliberation, important as it may be in

[1] See pages 33-7.   [2] See pages 37-42.
[3] See pages 45-53.
[4] Quoted by Sir Guilford L. Molesworth in, his Essay, *Silver and Gold : the Money of the World*. London and Manchester, 1891, pages 57. 58.

other respects, is one that lies at the very root of the difficulties of our Irish Land Question.

"Yet what can be plainer than that this is so? If the Bimetallist view, as I have stated it, is true, then progress on the lines of the present currency system means absolute ruin, sooner or later, to the whole body of the agricultural farmers of Ireland.

" Moreover, whether that view can be demonstrated to be sound or not, there is the significant fact that those twenty Governments have felt themselves called upon to send representatives to an International Congress for the consideration of it. That is quite enough for my present purpose.

"A danger which, even to the extent thus shown, has to be regarded as a possibly serious one, is surely not a thing to be left out of calculation. Hitherto, unfortunately, it has been almost absolutely left out of calculation in Ireland.

" Possibly the publication of this Interview may do something towards rousing from their present fatal lethargy, both the tenants themselves, and those who may have the responsibility of advising them when they are arranging terms of settlement, whether as tenants undertaking the obligation of a judicial rent, or as purchasers undertaking the obligation of repaying to the Government the purchase-moneys of their farms, principal and interest, by fixed yearly payments, for 49 years to come.[1]

" At all events, in the last resort, there remains the question from which I set out.[2]

" No responsible statesman who is not altogether ignorant of the facts of the case, as those facts are now

---

[1] See pages 2, 3, 8, 10.   [2] See Introduction. pages xi.-xiv.

admitted even by leading Monometallists themselves, will take upon himself the responsibility of saying that there is no need of providing a remedy for the unfortunate tenants who find themselves all but hopelessly encumbered by obligations of payments extending over prolonged terms of years—obligations now admittedly representing a burden altogether in excess of what was contemplated when their terms were fixed, or sanctioned, by the authority of the State itself.

" This, then, is the practical question :—

" Is nothing to be done to avert the disaster now plainly inevitable, if those whom recent legislation has subjected to the worst evils of our present currency system are left without a remedy ?"

www.ingramcontent.com/pod-product-compliance
Lightning Source LLC
Chambersburg PA
CBHW030621270326
41927CB00007B/1271